W9-BBT-536

# Hold the Press

.............................

# Hold the Press

## The Inside Story on Newspapers

John Maxwell Hamilton *and*
George A. Krimsky

Louisiana State University Press
Baton Rouge and London

Copyright © 1996 by Louisiana State University Press
All rights reserved
Manufactured in the United States of America
First printing
05  04  03  02  01  00  99  98  97  96    5  4  3  2  1

Designer: Laura R. Gleason

Typeface: ITC Garamond Book

Typesetter: Impressions Book and Journal Services, Inc.

Printer and binder: Thomson-Shore, Inc.

All drawings are by David Norwood.

Library of Congress Cataloging-in-Publication Data

Hamilton, John Maxwell.
    Hold the press : the inside story on newspapers / John Maxwell
Hamilton and George A. Krimsky.
        p.      cm.
    Includes bibliographical references and index.
    ISBN 0-8071-2057-X (alk. paper)
    1. Newspapers.    I. Krimsky, George A.    II. Title.
PN4731.H28      1996
070.4—dc20                                              96-2250
                                                         CIP

The paper in this book meets the guidelines for permanence and durability of the
Committee on Production Guidelines for Book Longevity of the Council on
Library Resources. ⊗

To Alissa, Maxwell, and Michael . . . the new generation
of newspaper readers (we hope)

I have actually heard it rumored that some people do not believe all they read in the newspapers! This indicates an awakening which, while it bodes ill for the old-fogy editor, augurs well for honest journalism.

—C. C. Hunt, nineteenth-century newspaperman

Were it left to me to decide whether we should have a government without newspapers or newspapers without a government, I should not hesitate a moment to prefer the latter. But I should mean that every man should receive those papers and be capable of reading them.

—Thomas Jefferson

You cannot be passive about citizenship or about journalism. A good newspaper will reward you only so far as you are devoted to reading it critically.

—David Broder

The news is the privilege which the customer enjoys, but it is also the crossword puzzle which he alone must solve.

—E. B. White

How to read the classic . . . has long been taught in the schools. But the great universal classic of the common people's reading—the newspaper—has been neglected.

—Carl Sandburg

# Contents

# Acknowledgments

Jeff Cowart, Louis Day, Everette Dennis, Elaine Durham-Otto, Michael Emery, Regina Hamilton, Paula Krimsky, Duncan McDonald, James Shelledy, Betsy Sprague, and Tom Winship read all or part of this book and provided valuable comment.

Carolyn Pione was the prime minister of this volume. Ms. Pione, a former Associated Press reporter undertaking graduate studies at Louisiana State University, hunted down telling facts and anecdotes, made substantial editorial improvements, and above all contributed ideas. We are indebted to her.

# Foreword

If once the newspaper was regarded as the most basic form of public communication aimed at a generic reader called "the Kansas City milkman" whose modern successor has been called "Jane or Joe Six-pack," that is no longer true. The "great leveler" newspaper of general circulation, aimed at everyone in general and no one in particular, is now part of a complex modern communications mix.

It is, in fact, the newspaper's universal character and appeal that make it a continuing fact of life even in the era of the information superhighway.

While some might suggest that the newspaper is a dinosaur in the Information Age, the last remnant of an old technology, such assumptions couldn't be more wrong. The newspaper is the most important organizing force for news and information in the world today. More than any other medium, the newspaper offers an inventory of information—a menu, if you will—that includes a broad array of news, hard and soft, of the community, the nation, and the world. It is multifaceted in its content, ranging from the most serious assessment of public affairs, such as politics and economics, to the most playful feature about an ordinary person doing something extraordinary. The newspaper surveys the territory, makes choices for its readers, and offers them satisfying fare.

A newspaper also has a personality, what some commentators call "brand-name recognition," so that its readers, whether regular or occasional, know what to expect. One of the reasons that the newspaper is as vital today as in times past when it was the only wheel in town is that it is the model for many new media ventures. People speak of the new electronic newspaper, the cyberspace newspaper, and the journalism of empowerment, knowing that the newspaper is

so well known and easily understood by all that any attempt to replace it must do so by fulfilling all of its functions in bringing information, opinion, entertainment, and advertising together in a single, easily retrieved, and presumably inexpensive package. To date, no effort
at creating the electronic newspaper has truly succeeded, and those
that are making the most headway are largely owned and run by
newspapers and newspaper people.

Journalism and newspapers may become more interactive over
time, wherein reader/viewer feedback is faster and more efficient,
but essentially the same organizing, sifting, and delivery process
must occur. The newspaper is the master teacher for the electronic
age, and nothing has yet surpassed it. In time, some futurists say, the
newspaper delivered on paper may disappear, but the functions of
the newspaper and its utility never will. Newspapers may become
more technologically advanced and reader-friendly, but some of their
fundamental contours and purposes will not likely change much in
the decades ahead.

Of course, the essence of the newspaper since it was first created
is dynamism and the ability to cope with change—change in the
world itself, change in journalistic styles and standards, change in
reader interests and passions. The newspaper is the master of change.
Unlike the horse and buggy of times gone by, which was replaced by
the automobile, the newspaper is leading and integrating with the
world of electronic images and satellite delivery. The newspaper is a
system, a news-gathering organization, substance and content, and an
influential force.

It is the growing complexity of the content of newspapers, radio
and television newscasts, and other sources of public communication
that has caused some observers to urge a "media literacy" movement,
or at least an effort to help readers and viewers better navigate and
understand the news and information directed at them from many
sources. For example, the *Wall Street Journal* carries so much complex material organized in various sections and departments that
there is a lengthy paperback guide to the paper and its content. Many
people wrongly assume that newspapers in general require little interpretation or few guideposts for the reader. That belief is wrong, as the
press follows the path of "market segmentation" and increasingly targets specific upscale readers and preferences—that is, those who are

well educated and mostly affluent. While it is still possible for any citizen to buy a paper on a newsstand, that is no guarantee he will fully understand and appreciate all he ought to know about that newspaper's purposes and content and be a truly discerning reader and consumer of news.

In this book, John Maxwell Hamilton and George A. Krimsky have produced an insider's guide to the newspaper (and other media) that is both accessible and readable. Blessedly, they have connected the "what you see" with the "what you get" aspects of the newspaper, and they make sense out of an increasingly dense thicket of news and other information carried by the typical newspaper in the United States. The book offers insights into the people who produce newspapers—their outlook, approach, and professional objectives—thus quashing many popular misunderstandings. The book also connects the content of the newspaper with the countinghouse—that is, its economic reasons for being and their implications. Here we get some inkling about the motivation of newspaper owners.

To understand the newspaper fully, readers need to know the rules of the game—the standards, style, and structure of the press, which this book provides. Knowing how and why stories are written is essential, as is the selection of news sources.

For anyone who has ever questioned why newspapers do what they do and what one can expect to see now and in the future, this book is essential. It was written by two distinguished news professionals with experience in leading newspapers and wire services in the United States and other parts of the world. Hamilton and Krimsky are now educators in the best sense: one is a dean of a leading school of journalism, and the other heads a respected training center for international journalists. Both have the benefit of vast international experience and often confront questions from visitors who have little understanding of the U.S. news environment. That gives them and their book a sharply focused sense of key questions in the minds of students, citizens, news professionals, international visitors, and critics of what one needs to know about newspapers, news people, and the news itself.

This book gives its readers a rich perspective filled with facts, analysis, interpretation, and good sense. While well aware of the work of critics and theoreticians, Hamilton and Krimsky deal in practicalities and bring the real world of journalism into focus. This book is an excellent text for students of journalism, communication, and media studies, as well as a useful guide for any citizen interested in demystifying the newspaper and the often puzzling nature of the news media.

EVERETTE E. DENNIS
Executive Director
The Freedom Forum Media Studies Center
at Columbia University

# Hold the Press

# Introduction: Why This Book?

Lord Beaverbrook, one of Britain's famous press barons, spoke aptly of the "black art of journalism." Publishers, editors, and reporters pull around their shoulders the mantle of high public service. They consider themselves a virtual branch of open, democratic government, the Fourth Estate. Yet the inner workings of the daily newspaper remain murky, even malevolent, to most readers.

We are among the many journalists who consider the newspaper business a higher calling. We believe the newspaper is the best way to get information to the public on a daily basis. But we do not think the black art of journalism produces gold out of the dross of daily events. Furthermore, we firmly believe that the public must be able to evaluate the news and its deficiencies if our press and our government are to work properly. That is the purpose of this book.

Journalists contribute to public ignorance about news gathering. Over a few drinks in the local bar they inevitably dissect the newsroom and criticize its shortcomings. But let someone from outside the fold sit down at the table and they are as tight-lipped and defensive as the most obdurate politician. Daily newspapers largely ignore their own industry in the news pages, and when they do cover it, they rarely probe very deeply. With mottoes on their front pages such as "All the News That's Fit to Print" (New York *Times*) and "The World's Greatest Newspaper" (Chicago *Tribune*), they have advertised themselves with all the puffery of old-time patent medicine salesmen.

Our schools are no better. They do far less to illuminate the workings of the daily newspaper than they do to explain the functioning of the White House or the local school board. "Most American college students," reports a study by the Freedom Forum Media Studies Center, "get little or no formal look at the media in their basic general

1

studies textbooks." While no one would think of allowing citizens to drive cars without a little instruction, the common assumption is that anyone can read a newspaper without understanding the rules and routines that shape its content.

Repeatedly, intelligent observers of the media have echoed Frederick Lewis Allen's comments three-quarters of a century ago in the *Atlantic Monthly:* "I should like to see lectures on 'How to Read the Newspapers' given in colleges and schools and elsewhere. . . . Only as we are able to estimate the relative amount of credence to be given to conflicting reports, and to judge for ourselves the reliability of the sources of the news, do we come somewhere near seeing that true picture of the world about us which we must see if we are to play our part in it intelligently and independently."

With the failure to rise to Allen's challenge, journalists lose credibility, readers are tempted to become nonreaders, and democratic government is undermined. The U.S. Constitution's protection of a free press was not designed primarily for journalists. It was designed for the citizens. To fulfill their role in a democratic society, citizens must have access to ideas and information. Journalists have cast themselves as special agents in this process, skilled at finding facts and presenting them to the public. But this skill comes to nothing if citizens don't know how to interpret what they find in their newspapers.

In one of the better studies of news gathering, *Reading the News,* Carlin Romano notes the importance of readers being active, not passive: "For *what* the press covers matters less in the end than *how* the public reads. Effective reading of the news requires not just a key—a Rosetta stone by which to decipher current clichés—but an activity, a regimen. It requires a tough-minded, pragmatic nose for both information and nuance that alerts the reader to when a new key is needed."

This book addresses this need. It is not to be confused with the many how-to manuals that either "sell" people on their newspapers or impart the bare essentials of reporting. Would-be journalists will learn something about mechanics of the craft. Newspaper subscribers will learn how to use their newspapers, even down to getting a letter to the editor in print. But the primary purpose that motivates this book is to help people *think* about their newspaper and what is in it. It is designed for those who want to understand the news.

Journalists have produced stacks of self-congratulatory, promotional literature violating their own standards for lively, searching examination. This does not appeal to us. We have pronounced views on what is wrong with journalism as well as on what it can do well. No one can understand the daily newspaper without appreciating the inherent limitations of providing information on rigid deadlines and in the small chunks called for in a constrained format. Nor can readers understand their newspaper without taking into account the artificiality of formulas for news reporting, including balance and other conventions used to contrive objectivity. Newspapers couldn't come close to telling readers everything they need to know even if space weren't constrained and reporters didn't make stupid mistakes that weren't compounded by a clumsy headline writer or copy editor. The motto of the New York *Times* notwithstanding, "All the reporters in the world working all the hours of the day could not witness all the happenings in the world," Walter Lippmann once noted.

Like the daily newspaper, this thin volume is not definitive. It is too short, and newspapers are too complicated.

Newspapers are simultaneously noble and plebeian. One of the best summations of the press's higher purposes came from the famous Commission on the Freedom of the Press in the 1940s. The commission identified five general services that the media provide: (1) an accurate, comprehensive account of the day's news in a context that gives it meaning; (2) a forum for the exchange of comment and criticism; (3) a representative picture of the constituent groups in society; (4) presentation and clarification of the goals and values of society; and (5) wide distribution of news. But coexisting with this deeply felt sense of public service is another role. Newspapers are a business. They make money for owners and are dedicated to selling products for advertisers, so much so that the amount of space available for news each day is determined by the number of ads, not the other way around. In space that the newspaper could use to provide hard news it offers readers a daily diet of horoscopes, comics, advice to the lovelorn, cute pictures, and other frivolous entertainment.

Given the freedom with which they do business, the nation's 1,550 odd daily newspapers and 7,400 plus weeklies are remarkably similar in content, format, and approach to reporting. Nevertheless, individual papers have personalities. Some appeal to a national audience; some are strictly local. The *Wall Street Journal* doesn't use any photos on its news pages, only line drawings; *USA Today* strives for engaging photos and lots of color to draw in readers. Journalism, as taught in universities, calls for relentless fact checking, yet some tabloids blithely report Martian visits and two-headed babies. Some newspapers are so determined to make money that they invest little in their editorial product; others spend considerable sums of money unearthing bad news about their advertisers.

What's more, conventions are changing. Worried about the future of their business, editors and publishers are experimenting with new techniques to grab readers, including shorter stories and more "news you can use." They are also delivering the news in new ways. In 1994 more than 600 daily papers sold voice services with current information on the weather, sports, and other news topics, and more than 140 dailies offered on-line computer access to full-text databases of their newspapers.

We believe the traditional ink-on-paper newspaper will continue to exist even as new technologies deliver the daily "newspaper" on-line. We also believe this time of transition makes it particularly important to understand the fundamental news process, what works well and what doesn't. For this reason, this book is more than a discussion of newspapers. It is a discussion of news.

In providing a broad perspective, this book draws sometimes from industry data, sometimes from anecdotes. While examples of design and management innovation often come from smaller papers, many examples of news coverage come from larger ones. Although the great mass of people read smaller local newspapers, the national and metropolitan newspapers set the industry standard for hard news reporting. Their shortcomings suggest general shortcomings.

This brings us back to the central purpose of this book. "For 150 years, journalists have sought success and power and respectability, usually in that order, and society has responded with unease and occasional hostility," press critic James Boylan has observed. We do not consider this tension between the public and the press to be bad, provided it rests on a sound understanding of what journalists can and cannot do well. The best watchdog of journalists is a knowledgeable, discriminating public.

# I

......................................

# The Calling of the Press

# Why the Press Does a Lousy Job Covering Subjects You Know a Lot About

At Louie's Cafe, people wander in for a cup of coffee on the way to work. Most open their newspapers. They scan for stories about their profession or for items that relate to their lives, say, the debate in the legislature about the state income tax. These they read closely. They also read other articles that catch their eye. An insurance agent looks at the story on increases in bank interest rates; a banker reads about the soaring costs of equipment for medical diagnosis. With these stories they glean the main points, but often don't probe with as much intensity.

This part of their daily routine done, they chat with each other. They inevitably complain about the stories they know most about, while showing far more acceptance of news about subjects in which they are not expert. The insurance agent dislikes the story on medical technology; it "skimmed the surface" on the implications for health insurance. The banker dislikes the article this morning on interest rates: "oversimplified."

And what of the newspaper editor who is also among the group? Some days he might also wade into the conversation and justify the paper's shortcomings. Today he just listens. After all, he thinks to himself, only a specialist in the newspaper business would understand that a newspaper wouldn't be doing its job if it wrote for specialists. The newspaper is for generalists.

The daily newspaper, like network television, general interest magazines, and other mass media, is designed for Everyman and Everywoman just the way stretch socks promise "one size fits all." Those

7

average readers juggle many obligations. On any given day they're hurrying to get the kids to daycare, fix the car, get groceries and make dinner, and still put in a full day of work. The last thing they want in a newspaper is stories they cannot quickly understand. To give these readers a wide range of information that can be consumed in a limited amount of time, newspaper journalists simplify the news. They leave the details, comprehensiveness, and complexity for the specialist publications.

Imagine, for instance, that Moses just came down from Mount Sinai with the Ten Commandments. The reporter who greets him at the bottom of the mountain has to file a story in an hour. The editors say it should run no more than eight hundred words. One of the obvious angles is to "lead" with *one* of the more newsworthy commandments, one that seems especially relevant at the moment. Another is to play down the commandments and play up the surrounding issues, for instance, that this intervention from God comes at a time when the Israelites, chased into the desert by the Egyptians, need all the help they can get. Either lead is bound to leave out a lot and certainly won't satisfy theologians.

A real-life example of compression was itself news in 1975. A Catholic bishop gave a 1,500-word sermon on five human rights listed by the Synod of Bishops in Rome. In the audience were President and Mrs. Ford. Owing to a faulty public address system, a wire service reporter mistakenly thought the bishop called on the president to "oppose abortion." Although the bishop devoted only a few words to the topic, abortion was then, as it is now, a touchy subject and, given the presumed comment directed toward the president, who is by definition newsworthy, the reporter considered this part of the speech the most important. A press critic later complained that the reporter should not have concentrated on the short reference to abortion. But concentration on a small part of an event happens all the time; this instance happened to be noteworthy only because the reporter got the facts wrong.

One technique for dealing with highly technical events is to tell people they occurred and gloss over the details altogether. This can be irritating to some readers, but sometimes the details just don't translate easily into a news story. For an example, consider the New York *Times* report on Fermat's last theorem.

Toward the end of his life, the seventeenth-century mathematician Pierre de Fermat noted in the margin of a book that he had found a solution to this theorem: "The equation $x^n + y^n = z^n$, where $n$ is an integer greater than 2, has no solution in positive integers." He never spelled out the solution, however, and for 350 years mathematicians labored over the problem. Then, in 1993, a British professor at Princeton came up with the answer. The *Times* bravely covered the event in a front-page story. The first 375 words of the article gave no details about the problem itself, let alone the solution. It concentrated instead on the human factor, that professional mathematicians were elated by the discovery. When the story got into the details of the theory itself, the reader hit a brick wall of technical language:

> Fermat's last theorem has to do with equations of the form $x^n + y^n = z^n$. The case where $n$ is 2 is familiar as the Pythagorean theorem that the squares of the lengths of two sides of a right-angled triangle equal the square of the length of the hypotenuse. One such equation is $3^2 + 4^2 = 5^2$, since $9 + 16 = 25$.
>
> Fermat's last theorem states that there are no solutions to such equations when $n$ is a whole number greater than 2. This means, for instance, that it would be impossible to find any whole number $x$, $y$ and $z$ such that $x^3 + y^3 = z^3$. Thus $3^3 + 4^3$ (27 + 64) = 91, which is not the cube of any whole number.

Even with all this detail, the story still did not explain the solution that had been developed, not that most readers cared. (Those who did—the mathematicians—had read all about it on the Internet in the arcane language they understood.) This mathematic discovery was big news. But some news does not fit the standard newspaper format.

As keen as journalists are to compress the news into manageable chunks, one form of simplification actually eats up space. Journalists often repeat themselves. The assumption is that readers don't have adequate background and need to be reminded of context. Thus, even when quoting a well-known senator, the reporter must not assume the reader remembers the legislator's state or party. Senator Ted Kennedy becomes Sen. Edward M. Kennedy (D-Mass). In the case of complex, ongoing stories, the reporter must supply even more standard information each day. During the bloody civil war in Rwanda in 1994, stories would have standard paragraphs like this: "The new fighting erupted after Rwanda's Hutu president, who had signed a peace agreement with the rebels, died in an unexplained plane crash April 6." The same situation prevails in local stories. In Associated Press bureaus, reporters keep a database of "nut graphs" to insert into ongoing stories. (Among other things, it saves reporters from having to look up the background or, worse, rely on their memories under deadline pressure.)

Compensating for this repetition, journalists use shorthand descriptions that save space *and* convey meaning. A reporter may note that such-and-such a senator is "liberal" or a "maverick." It became something of a joke that journalists made "powerful" the virtual first name of former representative Wilbur Mills, chairman of the House Ways and Means Committee.

Such shorthand avoids long-winded background that slows down the story and loses readers. But readers should also be wary of shorthand. If a murderer has served in the Marine Corps, reporters often draw attention to his being "a former marine." Rarely would a reporter highlight the military record of a murderer who served in the Coast Guard. The implication is that marines, by definition, are instinctive killers. Likewise, journalists summarized President Nixon's problems as "Watergate," referring to the building where Republican henchmen tried to steal Democratic party documents. Not bad shorthand, perhaps, but reporters soon ran amuck with "Koreagate," "Irangate," "Contragate," "Billygate," "Lancegate," "Nannygate," and other "gates," the details of which fade in memory because they are contrived.

Journalistic writing is scorned for "nudging, winking, and using four-letter words" in its attempt to make information digestible. This requirement of mass media prompted British novelist Evelyn Waugh to define "news" as "what a chap who doesn't care much about anything wants to read." True enough, the 115 million Americans who read a daily newspaper become exasperated by stories about which they are expert. But the newspaper is not written for experts. Specialized information they must get elsewhere. The newspaper, ideally, helps them learn about other subjects. Without mass media, the experts in Louie's Cafe would know a lot about their fields but little about each other's.

· · · · · · · · · · · · · · · · · · · · · · · · · · · · · · · · · · · · · · · · · · · · · · · · · · · · · · · · · · · · · · · · ·

## Aside: Accuracy, Accuracy, Accuracy

"Accuracy, accuracy, accuracy." Every journalism textbook underscores the famous statement Joseph Pulitzer posted at the New York *World.* In the words of one standard text: "All information is verified before it is used."

In practice this means much concentration on getting the little things right. "Please spell that name for me, ma'am. Is it S-M-I-T-H or S-M-Y-T-H-E? And please confirm that address." But even these facts are difficult to nail down. Gathering information quickly, the most hard-working reporter may transpose a number in that street address; an editor may inadvertently introduce a mistake. The potential for error is compounded in complex stories in which accuracy depends on selecting from many facts and introducing nuance.

Readers are best equipped to judge the accuracy of stories about which they have the most knowledge and experience. This, says Martin Mayer, is why studies usually show that readers "doubt the accuracy of local reporting, consider national news fairly accurate, and believe implicitly in international reporting."

......................................................................

## Why Journalists Don't Believe Their Mothers

"If your mother says she loves you, check it out." As much as any journalistic saying, this old, irreverent saw is the heartbeat of the profession. Trade in facts, not emotions. Don't be a believer. Look dispassionately for proof.

More than any other country's press system, the United States media are fact based. They strive for information that can be verified, whether on a police blotter or in a press conference transcript. In theory, reporters assigned a story do not set out looking for facts to support a conviction they already hold. They may go forth with a hypothesis, but they must test and retest it against evidence. "News reports should be free from opinion or bias of any kind," proclaimed the American Society of Newspaper Editors as long ago as 1923 in its "Canons of Journalism."

A longtime city editor at the Milwaukee *Journal,* Harvey Schwander, typified the facts-first mentality of journalism. One day a young, talented reporter, working near Schwander, took the story of an auto accident called in by a newsman in the field. The young reporter handed the crusty editor the first page, on which he had written the location of the story as Fond du Lac.

"I thought this accident was in Oshkosh," Schwander said.

"Oshkosh, Fond du Lac, what's the difference?" the reporter responded.

Schwander, red-faced, jumped up and pushed the young man toward the elevator door. He was never seen in the newsroom again.

In the search for facts and proofs, journalists sometimes fancy themselves scientists. And they have indeed looked to modern science and the scientific method for inspiration. "Have you ever stopped to think what it means when a man acquires the scientific spirit?" Walter Lippmann asked in the 1920s. "It means that he is ready to let things be what they may be, whether or not he wants them to be that way. It means that he has conquered his desire to have the world justify his prejudices."

The most basic journalism rules today relate to facts. But fact-based reporting was not always a hallmark of journalism. It emerged gradually. The rise of modern science was one factor, already mentioned. Another was commerce. Publishers saw that tapping into the mass market depended on providing impartial news. Instead of offering reports slanted to the commercial and political predilections of a narrow group of readers, mass-market newspapers provided something every reader could use: the facts.

Journalists, of course, can't be true scientists. Scientists are not expected to produce a new finding daily in uncontrolled environments and about subjects on which they are not expert. But this is what journalists do. They have rigid deadlines, which they meet in chaotic circumstances. And while a biologist would not presume to work on a physics problem, journalists are not supposed to be intimidated by lack of experience in an area. Being an amateur is a plus.*

Journalists also recognize that raw facts alone are not enough. Consider the gubernatorial race in which Jones says his plan will lower state income taxes by two hundred dollars a person. What if Jones simply fabricated this figure, and his plan would raise taxes? What

---

* In recent years newspapers have been more open to hiring experts. Large newspapers are more likely to have a reporter with a law degree covering the Supreme Court or foreign correspondents who can speak the language in the countries they are covering. (In the latter case, the newspaper will often send them to school before sending them abroad.) But newspapers that have experimented with experts are often disappointed, as was the *Wall Street Journal* a few years ago. The paper recruited a group of journalists who worked for specialist publications, thinking they would enrich coverage of those topics in the *Journal*. It turned out, though, that the specialists could not easily adapt to the *Journal*'s requirement to write for a general audience.

truth does the journalist convey by reporting exactly what Jones said? Journalists must make decisions about facts. In a celebrated story, a reporter received a handout from an American ambassador. "This is a god-dam lie," the journalist said, "and I refuse to send it to my paper."

"Facts don't wear their meanings on their sleeves," said philosopher John Dewey. But once journalists start to discuss those meanings, they open the door to perilous subjectivity. As noted by Elmer Davis, one of this century's great journalists:

> The good newspaper, the good news broadcaster must walk a tightrope between two great gulfs—on one side the false objectivity that takes everything at face value and lets the public be imposed on by the charlatan with the most brazen front; on the other, the "interpretive" reporting which fails to draw the line between objective and subjective, between a reasonably well-established fact and what the reporter or editor wishes were the fact. To say that is easy; to do it is hard.

Just as highwire artists carry a pole to help them maintain their balance, journalists have props to help them preserve their objective distance from news. Reporters might believe that their mothers love them, but they would never let on. Instead, they would say, "A reporter talked to a woman today who said she loved her child."

To many outside the profession these may seem silly contrivances or, worse, what one scholar has called "strategic rituals" that have little to do with true objectivity. But such conventions, however simplistic, set a tone for readers and for the reporters themselves. They remind both that the journalist's ultimate goal is to strive for accurate, unbiased news.

....................................................................

## Aside: Why You Get Both Sides of a Six-Sided Story

One of the fundamental journalistic rituals is "balance." Journalists do not report what one person purports to be the truth, however compelling that truth may seem. They gather varying opinions. So when it comes to reporting their mother's love, journalists quote the views of others who agree or disagree. In this way they earn the status of impartial observer.

The concept of balance nicely fits the adversarial nature of the American democratic system. During elections each candidate gets equal time to make a case for his or her candidacy. As in a court of law, someone alleged to have transgressed is allowed to refute the charge. With good reason the Federal Communications Commission, which monitors the electronic media, equates balance with fairness. But just as our legal system does not always achieve justice, neither does balance always promote truth.

First, balance can be unfair. Suppose a school principal is falsely accused of child abuse by a vindictive parent. The principal may have an opportunity to deny the charge, but the mere story, however balanced, has put a doubt in people's minds that was not there before. In the real world one side may be right and the other wrong. Giving equal weight to both sides may confuse the issue rather than clarify it. Journalists, however, find it difficult not to report both sides of stories for fear of seeming partial and, perhaps, being wrong.

Second, stories often have more than two sides. Constraints of time and space, however, encourage journalists to limit the number of viewpoints. The tendency is to find "dueling experts" who have staked out views at distant poles. The idea, media scholar Mitchell Stephens has observed, is that journalists chain opinions to their opposites as if hoping "that these beasts will annihilate each other." Hand-to-hand combat between the good guys and the bad guys adds a nice bit of human drama while contributing to a feeling that truth is discoverable. One side wins, the other loses. End of controversy. Most public policy issues, however, have many nuances and many experts with a different perspective.

## Why Journalists Cringe When Asked for Help

The American press has a proud tradition of crusading to expose injustice and campaigning to have it rectified. But it takes great pride in another tradition: independence from any cause or institution other than itself. How does one reconcile those two seemingly contradictory agendas?

In truth, they aren't reconciled. Crusading journalism and dispassionate journalism are two separate missions in the American press. Crusading occurs when a newspaper takes up a cause, for instance, the New York *Evening Post*'s battle against Tammany Hall in the late nineteenth century or, in the 1990s, the Montgomery *Advertiser*'s award-winning investigative series "Doctors Watching Doctors," which found "physicians who maim, molest and sometimes kill patients were allowed to continue practicing in Alabama." But these causes are not the norm. Day-to-day journalism is mostly preoccupied with reporting what happened today.

Journalists' feelings on this subject are complex and difficult to unravel. They like to feel they are helping society—but helping through balanced reporting and not by lending a hand to a particular interest. This is one reason they are more open to taking up the cause of weaker elements in society, who cannot lobby effectively. One journalism hero who is well remembered for helping the little guy is Scripps-Howard's roving reporter during World War II, Ernie Pyle. Pyle complained about the hand brakes on soldiers' jeeps, which resulted in a redesign by the manufacturer, and he suggested "combat pay," which Congress enacted. But just as often reporters suppress personal feelings altogether, as Malcolm Browne did during a famous Saigon news event during the Vietnam War. When a Buddhist monk protested government policy by burning himself to death, Browne took pictures. "Frankly, it never occurred to me to interfere," he said later. In the words of former Associated Press general manager Wes Gallagher, journalists "are in the business of reporting the news, not making it."

Another reason journalists tend to get sweaty palms when they are asked to help some cause or group is that over years of experience in dealing with fringe elements in our society they develop a sixth sense for spotting disingenuous motives and self-interest—or at least they think they do. With so many people importuning them every day, they become highly skeptical, if not cynical.

Most newspapers still maintain strict house rules on separating hard fact in the news columns from opinion and advocacy on the editorial pages. Leonard Downie, editor of the Washington *Post,* says he tries to avoid reading his own paper's editorials. He does not want to influence his on-the-merits approach to news coverage. This credo of dispassion was articulated nearly a century ago by New York *Times* publisher Adolph S. Ochs, who said his purpose was "to give the news impartially, without fear or favor, regardless of any party, sect or interest involved."

European journalists see their role differently. They believe it is their right to insert personal opinion and preference in the news columns. They aren't shy about using judgmental adjectives like "ridiculous" or "commendable." The continentals argue that journalism is more than a simple recording of events: it is a guide for public behavior and a stimulant to new thinking. In America, the daily press has traditionally left readers largely to fend for themselves when it comes to drawing conclusions from the information.

Now there are signs that both sides are moving closer to the other in thinking. In a data-hungry world, the Europeans are beginning to see the value of quickly delivered, unvarnished, reliable information. The Americans may be starting to see the value of engagement.

A new concept emerging around the country is public journalism. Newspapers are experimenting with ways to shed their role as arm's-length observers and become more involved in community concerns. "Public journalists want public life to work. In order to make it work, they are willing to declare an end to their neutrality on certain questions," says Jay Rosen, public journalism guru. He notes that the Wichita *Eagle,* the Charlotte *Observer,* and the Tallahassee *Democrat* "have redesigned their political coverage to emphasize the concerns of citizens rather than the maneuvers of candidates or the machinations of insiders." In Norfolk, Virginia, the *Virginian-Pilot* and *Ledger-Star* appointed a "public editor" and sponsored community discussions about crime.

Proponents of the movement do not advocate newspapers taking sides on controversial issues. Instead, they suggest furthering debate by highlighting possible solutions. Says media critic Martin Schram, "You don't have to crusade for any one new plan, because if you do that, there are winners and losers."

Still, ending neutrality and opening up news judgment to public scrutiny, many journalists believe, would put a newspaper on treacherous footing. Pulitzer Prize–winning journalist Richard Aregood considers public journalism to be heresy. "We are abandoning a piece of our own jobs if what we are doing is asking people what we should do." He is critical of using panels and focus groups to decide what should be covered, saying, "We may as well go into the mirror business."

Another reason traditional editors resist the activist role is that it opens up opportunities and temptations for abusing the truth. If you employ a reporter who sees wrongdoing under every rug or nurtures a personal cause (no matter how "good" it might be), that reporter tends to have the story's conclusion in mind before even looking for the information. And if the facts don't fit, out they go. That, to most newspaper editors in America, is still anathema.

# Why Journalism Is (or Isn't) a Profession

A political reporter discusses the implications of a campaign poll with the candidate's strategist. A business reporter talks about leveraged buyouts at a broker's cocktail party. A *Newsday* health and science reporter writes a stunning book on the global spread of infectious diseases.

For all their need to write for a general audience, reporters often are steeped in the subjects about which they write. They even become social and intellectual equals with those whom they cover. But does this mean journalists qualify as professionals?

The question has been debated in American newsrooms and classrooms for more than a century. In many occupations the categorization is clear. Automobile assembly-line workers practice trades. Doctors and lawyers practice professions. But these categories do not work for journalists.

The Constitution, from which journalists draw their reason for being, offers little help in defining the status of the press. The First Amendment states what government cannot do: "Congress shall make no law . . . abridging freedom of speech, or of the press." It does not say what journalists can or should do. That has been an evolutionary process shaped by social needs, technological advances, and commercial considerations.

One battleground for the debate is the terrain on which journalists are trained. Journalism schools have never found a comfortable niche on college campuses. Journalism faculties war over emphasizing analytical reasoning and theory or practical skills like editing. Practicing journalists ridicule journalism research as abstract and irrelevant, while the general mind-set in universities favors specialized analysis. Journalism educators typically describe their programs as professional schools. Other academics derisively refer to them as trade schools.

As the campus debate suggests, there is no discrete or specialized body of knowledge whose mastery is required to practice journalism. Editors acknowledge this in their hiring practices. According to a 1992 survey, only 39 percent of all journalists have majored in some field of communications. By some counts 20 percent have no degree at all. More to the point, a journalism degree is not a very good predictor of success in the field. Many journalists with college training in the humanities, business, or social sciences excel, and in many cases editors prefer to hire them over journalism-school graduates.

Those who say journalists are not professionals argue that journalists are not licensed as are doctors and lawyers. The American Medical Association and the American Bar Association police their own ranks. While journalists have professional organizations, none has policing power. Journalists can't be disbarred. As much as journalists want to be viewed as professionals, they balk at enforceable codes of ethics. Such codes would suggest possible limits to constitutional guarantees of free speech, and none could adequately cover the complex realities faced daily in reporting news.

Yet journalism is more than an occupation like selling shoes. It is a calling, as are law and medicine, with many shared assumptions about serving the public good. As is apparent throughout this book, journalists tend to describe their daily work in terms of values rather than as techniques. While they do not like binding codes of ethics, journalism organizations spend considerable time discussing accuracy, fairness, and other values; they measure each other's work by these standards. Also like other professionals, journalists conserve the status quo. They close ranks to protect comrades who stay more or less within established norms and to chastise those who stray from them.

The ambiguity of defining journalists is complicated further by their odd relationship to the news *business*. In the words of a famous study on the media, "Journalism is a profession grafted on to an industry." As the *Nation* editorialized in 1879, "If journalism is a profession, there is one respect in which it is very different from other professions—that it is closely connected with, and dependent upon, commercial enterprise; that it involves the use of a large amount of fixed capital." The sine qua non of newspapers, said the *Nation*, was circulation, and editorial values serve that profitable goal.

The *Nation*'s ultimate conclusion that journalism is not a profession, however, was based ultimately on something else. Unlike lawyers and doctors, journalists then toiled anonymously. "It is established as well as anything can be established by experience that the power of the press is in exact ratio to the strictness with which the incognito of its writers is preserved. . . . [Journalism] must seem always to be the loud, unanswerable voice of public opinion, and not that of some enterprising young journalist."

Much has changed since the *Nation* came to that conclusion. Today's "enterprising young journalists" have bylines and are visible community personalities, writing columns and attending social events. Readers are more likely to see the newspaper as a human, fallible institution. Meanwhile, the media is a bigger business than ever. The New York *Times* devotes its business section to the media industry every Monday.

The great paradox in this unresolved debate is that journalists' product is essential to democracy. But their high calling notwithstanding, journalists are hired hands in an industry that makes a lot of money. For journalists, this is a scab they can't help picking.

# II

.................................

# The Business

# Why There's a Bottom Line to News

Newspapers in the United States are a business and a highly profitable one at that. This is not to say that editors and reporters have both eyes on the bottom line whenever they chase a news story. As will be discussed in a subsequent section, American journalists are far less inclined to hew to owners' interests than journalists in the Communist-run Soviet Union were to follow the party line. But business considerations do shape the paper. To understand how, one must first understand the profit motive in newspapers.

"For most of the history of American journalism," historian Daniel Boorstin argues, "the independence and high quality of the American press have been tied . . . to the commercial spirit and the need to offer his money's worth to a purchaser in the open market." In colonial times entrepreneurial printers aimed to sell practical information to the public, particularly commercial news for the merchant class.

Although mass-market–based journalism has colonial antecedents, newspapers in Ben Franklin's era often appealed to narrow, elite interests. This was reflected in the papers' prices. In the early nineteenth century big New York papers sold for six cents a copy, a large sum in those days. According to consumer price indices, a citizen with six cents in 1820 had more buying power than a citizen with $1.20 in 1991.

The elitist press faded in the mid-nineteenth century, however, with the arrival of the penny press—that is, newspapers that sold for a single cent. The guiding idea behind this low-cost daily newspaper was to reach a wide audience that was increasingly literate and itself a market for other commercial products. The New York *Sun,* one of the pioneering penny papers, had this to say in its maiden issue in 1833:

"The object of this paper is to lay before the public, at a price within the means of everyone, all the news of the day, and at the same time afford an advantageous medium for advertising." To underscore this attitude, the *Sun*'s slogan was "It Shines for All."

As the press system has matured, a strong link has been forged between readership and advertising. The price charged for an ad is determined by the size of the audience the newspaper reaches. Knowing the exact audience size is so crucial to advertisers that most newspapers permit the Audit Bureau of Circulation to make an independent count.

Determined to maintain high circulations, newspapers have kept the cost to readers relatively low. As a result, the average American newspaper earns about 20 percent of its revenue from sales to readers and 80 percent from advertisers.* Despite competition from other media, newspapers still command a large share of the total dollars spent on advertising (more than $30 billion).

Newspapers are profit machines, "the most profitable legal business in America," says former Chicago *Tribune* editor James Squires. The newspaper divisions of publicly owned media companies, which account for about one-third of total national daily circulation, had profit margins of 16.5 percent in 1990. That is to say that those newspapers earned more than 16 cents profit on each dollar of revenue. This is all the more remarkable because 1990 was a time of steep downturn in the economy. In 1985 newspapers were earning more than 20 cents profit on each dollar of revenue. In comparison, most other industries are delighted with 10 percent or even 5 percent profit margins. In 1990 the median profits of Fortune 500 industrial companies was 4.1 percent.

Newspaper owners do what all business people do: try to protect profits and support laws and regulations that suit the bottom line. Publishers were in the forefront of fighting child labor laws that made it more difficult to use newsboys, and they have fought for government postal subsidies. They have also tended to be antilabor and have shown a killer instinct in trying to put competing newspapers out of business. In this respect they have been quite effective.

---

  * The 20 percent of revenue that comes from subscribers is about equal to the cost of delivering the newspaper. As former publisher Nancy Hicks Maynard has pointed out, this means that the news in the newspaper is free to the reader, who pays only for delivery.

The number of daily newspapers has steadily dropped. In 1900 the United States had more than 1,950 dailies. In 1950 it had 1,772. Today it is closer to 1,550. Only thirty-three United States cities have competing newspapers, also a steep drop from fifty years ago when seventy-three cities had separately owned newspapers battling for circulation.

The successful newspapers have thrived. While the total number of papers is down, the combined circulation of all dailies is up from 50 million in 1950 to 59 million in 1994. The average circulation in 1900 was 7,500; today it is above 35,000.

This decline in competing newspapers and the rise in average circulations is all part of a larger trend toward big corporate news operations. Larger-than-life newspaper tycoons like William Randolph Hearst and Joseph Pulitzer dominated the early days of mass-market newspapers. Today's leaders are still sometimes colorful and can amass personal fortunes, but they are less and less likely to be sole owners and much more likely to be executives supervising large corporations and guarding stockholders' interests (and dividends).*

Sibling friction and changes in U.S. inheritance laws have driven families to sell their papers, and the earning power of newspapers has driven corporations to snap up these lucrative holdings. In 1900 less than 2 percent of all daily newspapers were part of a group. Today the chances are three to one that the newspaper you read is owned by a group, a bland term preferred over *chain* by corporate executives. Thomson Newspapers, the largest, had more than 108 in 1995; Gannett, second with 82 newspapers, also owns television and radio stations and a billboard advertising company. Knight-Ridder Newspapers Inc., Cox Newspapers, New York Times Company, Times Mirror Company, Newhouse Newspapers Group, and many others have large holdings as well. "There are fourteen dominant companies that have half or more of the daily newspaper business (seven years ago there were twenty)," press critic Ben Bagdikian observed in 1992.

---

* It should also be noted that newspaper groups are also offering the same high financial incentives to their top executives as other big companies do theirs. When Gannett chairman and CEO Al Neuharth retired in 1989, he left with company stock worth more than $20 million, an annual pension of about $700,000, and deferred salary payments of about $200,000 a year for the rest of his life, plus a few other goodies.

One of those who decried commercial-based journalism was Upton Sinclair. Sinclair's comments in *The Brass Check: A Study of American Journalism,* self-published in 1919, perceptively presaged the direction of the newspaper business through this century:

> A modern newspaper is an enormously expensive institution. The day is past when a country printer could set up a hand-press and print news about the wedding of the village blacksmith's daughter and the lawn-party for the Christian Endeavor Society. . . . The franchise which entitles a paper to this news from all over the world is very costly; in most cities and towns it is an iron-clad monopoly. You cannot afford to pay for this service, and to print this news, unless you have a large circulation, and for that you need complicated and costly presses, a big building, a highly trained staff. Incidentally you will find yourself running an advertising agency and a public employment service; you will find yourself giving picnics for news-boys, investigating conditions in the county-hospital, raising subscription funds for a monument to Our Heroes in France. In other words, you will be an enormous and complex institution, fighting day and night for the attention of the public, pitting your composite brain against the other composite brains in the struggle to draw in the pennies of the populace.

Sinclair called his book *The Brass Check* because visitors to houses of prostitution in his time bought a brass check at the door, which they gave to the woman whose favors they sought. Journalists, Sinclair argued, were prostituted to business. While many dispute that, it is true that commercial interests do shape aspects of the news product and very often in ways that are not at first apparent.

## Why the Reader Can Profit from a Profitable Newspaper

During the early 1990s the Times Mirror Company cut costs. With advertising down sharply and the price for newsprint up drastically, its flagship newspaper, the Los Angeles *Times,* killed its San Diego County edition, its *Sunday City Times* section, aimed at inner-city readers, and its special World Report published each Tuesday. It initiated several waves of "buyouts" to reduce the size of the staff. In 1995 management also axed two of the corporation's financially weak newspapers, the *Evening Sun* in Baltimore and New York *Newsday,* a Pulitzer Prize–winning newspaper that had lost an estimated $100 million during the decade it was in operation.

The architect of the 1995 cuts was Mark Willes, Times Mirror president and CEO. Earlier in the year he had come to the company from General Mills. Reporters referred to him ruefully as Cap'n Crunch. But all journalists understood that once you have built a system around commerce, the profitability of a newspaper plays a large role in determining how good the product is. As Times Mirror's actions show, lower revenue limits the number of sections and the size of the editorial staff, and even threatens the ultimate survival of the newspaper itself. One reason book review sections in Sunday newspapers have decreased in recent years is the reduction of advertising by book publishers.

Salaries and newsprint, in that order, are the two biggest items in the newspaper budget. Paper prices alone account for about 20 percent of the budget of many newspapers. When paper prices began to soar in late 1994, the newspaper industry reeled. The Brattleboro *Reformer,* circulation 10,000, decided to charge families $50 for running biographical information with an obituary of a dearly beloved. The Vermont paper "did not start charging for obits in order to get rich," the editor told readers; "it did so to stay above water." The Houston *Post* folded. "The *Post* got hit in the head with a roll of newsprint," said William Dean Singleton, president and chief executive of the parent company, Consolidated Newspaper Inc.

The need to make money limits a newspaper. But judging just how unsatisfactory the profit motive is requires one to consider how much better or worse the alternatives might be. Upton Sinclair, a socialist, worried about the capitalist basis of the press, foreseeing the dilemma that faced the Los Angeles *Times.* But Sinclair did not spell out an alternative media system, perhaps because, as Walter Lippmann suggested, Sinclair "cannot convince anybody, not even himself, that the anti-capitalist press is the remedy for the capitalist press." A state-owned press may not have to worry about profits, but dealing with a government master is even more troubling. How can the press be a check on the government when it works for the government?*

---

* There are examples of government-owned or -financed media producing first-rate news. The British Broadcasting Corporation is one example. But these work in a culture of predominantly private-sector funding, which sets the standard for what is acceptable and what isn't. Even though the U.S. government funds public television and radio, any attempt to intervene in its programming is sure to set off a controversy.

"The more successful a newspaper is commercially, the better for its moral side," Joseph Pulitzer said. "The more prosperous it is, the more independent it can afford to be . . . the less subject it will be to temptation, the better it can stand losses for the sake of principle and conviction."

While some critics argue that such heavy dependence on advertising distracts newspapers from the interests of their readers, advertising also has an arguably positive influence on objectivity in the news pages. For all their own interest in hype, advertisers want newspapers to be factual and honest, as journalism educator Philip Meyer has noted: "Truth is what the customers pay for—readers directly and the advertisers indirectly because they want their own messages to appear in a credible environment." The most irresponsible advertisers, he adds, use irresponsible newspapers like the sensational *National Enquirer,* which sells in supermarkets with stories such as "Aunt's Psychic Dream Saves Missing Teen."

"If the front page announces that a housewife was impregnated by a border collie, look inside and check the ads," Meyer writes. "You will find that the only ones there are addressed to people who will believe anything, e.g., that there are pills that can make you lose weight while you sleep."

Just as journalists and media critics often ignore the connection between the quality of news and the quality of advertising, they forget that advertising is a public service in its own right. You, the newspaper reader, may ignore tire ads 364 days of the year, but on the day you need to buy new tires, that may be the sole reason you read the paper. Advertisers pay to put ads in newspapers because consumers read them.

Some even say that advertisers have promoted readability. Colonial advertisers, note media historians Michael and Edwin Emery, "quickly discovered that their messages must be simply stated to reach the most people. . . . Advertisers also understood the value of attractive presentation. They led the way in experimentation with type, illustrations, make up, and legibility. The press owes much to these practical psychologists and graphics artists."

Large, profitable newspaper groups can better afford to pay for high-cost news-gathering operations such as those costly foreign bureaus. But bigness and profits don't automatically lead to more enterprise on the news side. Ralph Ingersoll, Jr., who owns a chain of more than thirty newspapers, has claimed he can raise profit margins on revenue to thirty-eight cents on the dollar. The trade-off, however, is costly for the quality of the news operation.

The process of becoming big has drawbacks as well. Newspapers must earn profits to pay off the debts incurred in acquiring new properties, many of which are bid up to high levels. "You can [pay] two or three times the gross revenues of a healthy newspaper in a healthy market and continue to publish a good one. But some groups are paying five, six, and seven times revenues, and that usually forces cost cutting that kills editorial quality," says Jim Ottaway, Jr., chairman of Ottaway Newspapers Inc., which is now owned by Dow Jones, publisher of the *Wall Street Journal.*

Companies whose stock is publicly traded feel additional pressures to make profits. "Wall Street didn't give a damn if we put out a good paper in Niagara Falls," says former Gannett CEO Al Neuharth. "They just wanted to know if our profits would be in the 15–20 percent range."

This emphasis on profits shows up in Gannett's corporate mission statement, or "game plan," written by Neuharth's successor, John Curley, and updated annually. The first version, written in 1989, gave "as a first priority increased profitability and increased return on equity and investment." Not until 1992 did the plan mention that "we show respect for the First Amendment and our responsibility to it." It was last on the list of operating principles. Leaving out this news concern previously was an oversight, Curley explained; its belated inclusion came about because of criticism that Gannett's *USA Today* was too soft in its reporting.*

In 1995 two of the nation's leading editors resigned from newspapers owned by large media groups. Geneva Overholser, editor of Gannett's Des Moines *Register,* and Richard Aregood, editorial page editor of Knight-Ridder's Philadelphia *Daily News,* cited a lament heard in

---

* It is perhaps of more than passing interest that more socially uplifting mission statements are found in organizations outside the news business, for instance, United Parcel Service and Hallmark. Hallmark's mission statement begins, "We believe that our products and services must enrich people's lives and enhance their relationships." Gannett's 1989 version began, "To make acquisitions in news, information, and communications and closely related fields, like entertainment or advertising, that make economic sense."

newsrooms across the country. "I don't know a newspaper editor who is not frustrated by profit pressure at public companies," said Overholser, who was later hired as ombudsman at the Washington *Post.* "You're just constantly cost cutting."

"There's no question that most newspapers have become much more bottom-line oriented, even the ones we think of as quality newspapers," says William Winter, executive director of the American Press Institute. When newspapers need to maximize profits, they don't trim advertising sales or the circulation department as a rule; they hit the newsroom budget.

But the newspaper owners we prefer are the ones who realize profitability depends on news quality. Editorial integrity and financial health work together. A strong editorial "product" attracts readers, which is just what advertisers want. Faced with declining circulation in the mid–1960s, the New York *Herald Tribune* did not act boldly to improve its news content. "I wouldn't have tried to save the *Tribune* by cosmetics and typographical tricks," said Ivan Veit, New York *Times* business executive. "They never supported what they had, either internally with sufficient staff or externally with adequate promotion and personnel to build circulation. Instead, they nickel-and-dimed it to death."

## Why Journalists Don't Write Stories to Sell Newspapers

"Sure, I know why the reporter wrote that story. To sell newspapers."

There is no more common complaint about the press. The implication is that the marketplace drives journalists to write stories that run counter to their better instincts. Judging from the profit motive that inspires owners, one might assume this is a fact. It isn't. A reporter doesn't think about selling newspapers when sitting down to write a story any more than a major league batter thinks about the law of gravity when swinging at a fast ball. Good reporters might be good for business, but they are not particularly bottom-line oriented.

When the editors of the New York *Times* met with executives on the business side to agree on a statement of values for the paper, they ended up in heated debate over news and profits. An exasperated Max Frankel, the top editor at the time, spoke out forcefully. "A writer or an editor is judged by the brilliance of his journalism, even if it costs too much—especially if it costs too much. A business manager is judged by how he cuts costs and makes profits."

Journalists adopt this attitude quickly. When a newspaper hires a new reporter, the business side may determine the pay, but the selection of the employee is a newsroom decision, not a business one. It is rare when a reporter is even exposed to the paper's circulation or ad sales department during the interview process. And no self-respecting editor (or publisher, for that matter) would dare assign a story to a cub reporter with the admonition, "We're in the business to make money. Now, go out there and make me some."

Of course, newspapers depend on selling their product to advertisers and the public. There would be few travel stories if the travel industry weren't eager to advertise in Sunday travel sections. Ditto for grocery stores and food sections. In the same way, community newspapers announce weddings not because owners think it is particularly newsworthy but because readers like to see their names and the names of neighbors in the newspaper and are more inclined to buy a newspaper if those names are there.

Newspapers also are not diametrically opposed to pleasing advertisers in the content and placement of news. Where legitimate business news exists, for instance, the opening of a new mall, they generally go out of their way to ensure that it is covered. They agree not to run airline ads near news of an air crash or sometimes even agree to automatically switch the ads to another day.

But what about shaping the content of news stories to please advertisers or even ignoring news that will offend them? No doubt about it, advertisers exert pressure. The publisher and the business side feel it most often, but that pressure can reach into the newsroom. Sometimes it makes a difference in what appears as news, but the predominant sentiment in the business is that it isn't supposed to, ever.

In recent years, notes the *American Journalism Review,* the San Jose *Mercury News,* the Hartford *Courant,* the St. George (Utah) *Spectrum,* the Birmingham *News,* and the New Haven *Register* have "all bowed to the wrath of [auto] dealers" after running stories on how to get a good price on a car. In the face of a 1994 boycott by about forty advertisers, costing the *Mercury News* at least $1 million, publisher Jay Harris issued an apology for the paper's story. When the boycott continued, he ran a full-page house ad listing "10 reasons why you should buy or lease your next new car from a factory-authorized dealer."

Just how to assess the significance of advertising pressure is open to different interpretations. In a 1992 survey, nine out of ten newspaper editors were aware of advertisers trying to influence the news by threatening to remove their ads or actually doing so; more than one-third reported that such action was successful. On the other hand, former journalist and now journalism professor Philip Meyer has calculated that "the newspapers where such intervention happens more than once or twice a year reach only 14 percent of the total newspaper audience." Journalism critic Ben Bagdikian cites a 1980 study by the American Society of Newspaper Editors, which found that one-third of the editors working for newspaper chains did not feel free to run damaging stories about their own companies. Others, however, consider it remarkable that two-thirds did feel free to run negative stories. From their point of view, journalism is one of the only businesses in the world where the customer, not to mention the boss, isn't always right.

Large newspapers are best able to deal with angry advertisers. The advertiser is less likely to be the editor's neighbor and, in any case, probably needs the paper more than the paper needs the advertiser. Small papers are more vulnerable. A Pennsylvania weekly editor was once told he could run a story about purse snatchings at a local hardware store, which also happened to be a large advertiser. But the publisher warned that if the store pulled its advertising as a result, the editor would be out of a job. Nothing personal, but without the ad revenue the weekly simply couldn't stay in business. (The editor ran the story, naming the store but focusing more on the crime than on the location; no advertising was pulled.)

Concerted advertising pressure can also backfire. It's not good public relations. The advertiser boycott of the San Jose *Mercury News* prompted an antitrust investigation by the Federal Trade Commission. It ruled that the advertisers conspired to restrain trade and deprive "consumers of truthful information" by withdrawing ads. The FTC ordered the dealers to end the boycott.

Newsroom morale plummets when a publisher strolls into the editor's office and asks for special handling of a story relating to an advertiser. Reporters balk at puffing advertisers; and when they uncover something negative about one of them, they expect that the bad news will be published.

Journalists will often circle the wagons when they feel the "bean counters" on the business side are trespassing. When the *Mercury*

*News* ran that ad to appease auto dealers, the angry editorial staff sent so many E-mail messages over the newsroom network that the computer system crashed. Tony Moura, a New Haven *Register* copy editor, had a similar experience. He was overseeing editorial copy for a special auto section and included a wire service piece telling readers how to avoid paying sticker prices for cars. Local car dealers protested. When Moura was suspended for two weeks without pay, the staff took up a collection to cover his lost wages. News of the episode leaked to the *American Journalism Review,* which like other publications following the media loves to report transgressions.

Highly publicized episodes like this become object lessons for senior editors and publishers. Not wanting bad news about themselves, they learn to be chary about intruding into the newsroom on behalf of advertisers.

Journalists believe they should be separated from owners the way our Constitution mandates a separation of church and state. This contributes to antimanagement biases. A former dean of the Columbia University School of Journalism counseled his would-be journalists to have a small financial reserve set aside so they could tell wayward owners to go to hell. "The marketing language is not one that appeals to most journalists, who do not want to think of themselves as sellers or promoters of a product," said New York University journalism professor Jay Rosen. So different is the reporters' orientation from the publishers', press critic A. J. Liebling joked long ago, that they "usually root against their employers [in their choices in an election], and they are depressed when their paper has a winner."

Examples of this attitude abound. A 1994 study of larger dailies looked at twenty factors that could influence reporters to use one source over another. Pressure from advertising departments and a newspaper's policy on political issues ranked at the bottom in importance. A classic example of business interests being separated from editorial interests is an editorial that appeared in the New York *Times* on July 31, 1995. It criticized a House-passed telecommunications bill for narrowing ownership of news organizations, "even though large media companies, including The New York Times Company, could benefit."

The them-and-us attitude that pervades newsrooms can lead to practical headaches for publishers. We know of a medium-sized southern newspaper where the editor didn't want the advertising department to use photographs taken by the news staff. The argument: ad employees alter photos, which undermines the credibility of the newspaper. The publisher didn't see the problem. No one expects the same standards for ads as for news; besides, it is impossible to control ad photos since most are supplied by ad agencies. But the publisher also had to deal with newsroom concerns while still getting photos to illustrate special advertising supplements. He solved the problem by agreeing that news photos could not be used for promotion, but also that photographers could take pictures for the business side of the operation—and those couldn't be used on the news pages.

The idea of "reporters writing news to sell newspapers" is often taken to mean that reporters try to find stories that readers want to read. Naturally every journalist wants his or her story read, but most readers would be surprised how little time reporters devote to scoping out what the public wants. Reporters assume the reader likes the same things they do. In a famous study of newsroom attitudes, sociologist Herbert Gans looked chiefly at CBS, NBC, *Time,* and *Newsweek,* but his conclusions apply to newspapers as well: "I began this study with the assumption that journalists, as commercial employees, take the audience directly into account when selecting and producing stories. . . . I was surprised to find, however, that they had little knowledge about the actual audience and rejected feedback from it. . . . Instead, they filmed and wrote for their superiors and for themselves."

The recent trend toward group ownership, as well as evidence of declining readership, has encouraged management to think harder about readers' interests. Chain management has shown increasing propensity to staff newspapers with hometown talent who know the local scene. Chains are also careful to leave news decisions to local publishers and editors.

This same attitude goes for the editorial page, where owners have traditionally promoted their own views. A recent survey by the publishers' trade group the Newspaper Association of America asked 205 newspapers who decided which presidential candidate the paper endorsed. In 98.5 percent of the instances reported, owners left the decision to subordinates, usually the editorial board. In the case of group owners, the subordinate who made the decision wasn't on the business side either; it was the editor. Publishers and CEOs made the decision about 30 percent of the time.

The separation of church and state at newspapers has great value as far as quality of coverage is concerned. A healthy tension exists when reporters, with their own credos, pressure publishers and owners for more space and resources to cover stories. Without that pressure owners are often less inclined to provide decent coverage. When the owner of the Milwaukee *Journal* (now the *Journal Sentinel*) created an employee ownership plan for the newspaper (he hated unions, and this was a way to avoid dealing with them), the news employees acted like owners everywhere. In the interest of profits, they cut back on out-of-state bureaus.

......................................................................

## Aside: Newspaper Standards

Commerce is so much a part of the newspaper profession that a paper's quality is often judged in marketplace terms like "ad ratio." Responsible papers are thought to devote no more than 65 percent of their content to ads (the average is just under 60 percent). News staff sizes usually are pegged to circulation, with the standard being one employee for every 1,000 readers. By this standard, a newspaper with a circulation of 50,000 should have at least 50 reporters and editors.

In a review of industry trends during 1992, Scripps-Howard reported the following averages:

• The typical newspaper was divided more or less equally between editorial copy and advertising.

• Seventy-two percent of total circulation was home delivery; 28 percent was single copy sales.

• Sixty-five percent of newspapers were delivered by adult carriers, 35 percent by youth carriers.

• Fifty-two percent of ad revenue was local retail, 35 percent classified, and 13 percent national.

• For every 1,000 in its circulation, the average newspaper had 1.1 to 1.2 newsroom employees.

• Nineteen percent of beat reporters covered sports, 13 percent general assignment, 13 percent government and politics, 8 percent family and lifestyle, 7 percent business, 6 percent arts and entertainment, 4 percent education, 4 percent social issues, 4 percent police and crime, 4 percent courts. The remaining 16 percent covered other subjects.

• Seventy-six to 80 percent of the average newsroom budget covered employee costs, 10–15 percent covered features and wire/supplement services, and 2–5 percent paid freelance costs.

• An average of 2.3 adults read each copy of a newspaper.

......................................................................

# Why Journalists Sell Stories

The previous section noted that journalists aren't motivated by the thrill of selling newspapers. They are, however, motivated by the thrill of getting their stories into the newspaper. This is not bad for the reader, for it promotes interest and readability. But when pizzazz crosses a certain ill-defined line, it is called in the trade "hyping stories."

Reporters want to see their stories in the newspaper, preferably published with their bylines. To achieve this, they know they have to "sell" the editor on the value of the story. That means making the story compelling. This is an honorable objective, one almost as old as journalism itself. A reporter whose stories never run on the front page is like a ball player who never starts in a game.

A reporter can sell a story in different ways: through its intrinsic content (the reporter zeros in on that aspect of the news that is the most important and interesting) or by writing the story so well that the editor can't ignore it.

Talent and a "nose for news," as the old saying goes, help a reporter find a good story, but journalists also know tricks to pull the most out of a news event. Illustrative of this is the apocryphal story about a newsroom wit who began all his stories with: "In another front-page development today . . ."

Editors laugh off such techniques while applying the proverbial red pencil to the copy. But they appreciate journalists with surging competitive juices. Those juices push reporters to stretch for the big stories. Ben Bradlee, the retired editor of the Washington *Post,* liked to talk about reporters with "fire in their belly" and often pitted them against one another in the interest of getting the most out of them.

Readers are generally well served by journalists who fiercely compete to get the news and write it compellingly, provided the journalists don't depend on sensationalism or hype.

Sensationalism is difficult to avoid. The best newspapers claim they do not sensationalize. Yet the arrest of a celebrity for murder inevitably sets off a competitive war among the great mass of journalists for the hottest version. Hype is a greater sin. (The word is short for hyperbole, intentional exaggeration.) An example would be a reporter so playing up the provocative part of the news that reality about the event is distorted.

Just because journalists don't sell stories to editors in order to make money for the publisher doesn't mean publishers don't appreciate the reader interest that is generated. It all comes down to the same thing from the point of view of management: eager readers and profits.

It does not follow, though, that the more a paper veers toward sensationalism the greater the flow of black ink onto the company's ledgers. The sensationalist tabloid New York *Post* lost money for more than a decade. One reason was its loss of the upscale market. When former *Post* owner Rupert Murdoch tried to persuade advertisers not to defect, a department store spokesman is supposed to have replied: "But, Mr. Murdoch, your readers are our shoplifters."

# III

·······························

## The Look of the Newspaper

# Why Some News Is "Below the Fold"

A newspaper is a sort of daily encyclopedia. But whereas encyclopedias arrange information alphabetically, newspapers at first glance seem devoid of an organizing principle. Organization nevertheless does exist. Editors and the people who help them with design each day have formulas for attracting readers to the paper and then pulling them inside its pages. Knowing how to read the layout of a newspaper can be as useful as knowing how to interpret the individual stories themselves.

Start with page one.

Editors have established an elaborate hierarchy for placing stories. The main story in the standard broadsheet newspaper runs in the upper right-hand corner of page one.* In the old days that was where the big banner headlines running the full width of the front page screamed out some earthshaking event to attract the attention of a would-be customer. Street sales are no longer so important, but as noted previously, tradition dies hard in the news business. "Above the fold" is of a higher order than "below the fold" for the simple reason that stories on the top half of the front page are visible when newspapers are stacked up or displayed in a vending machine.

* The typical broadsheet measures 14 × 22 inches. The other standard format is the tabloid, which is smaller and presents different design considerations. Perhaps most important is that it is difficult to get more than one story on a page with an ad. At various times in history other page sizes have been tried. In the mid–nineteenth century some publishers experimented with "blanket" newspapers, which measured 3 × 5 feet. This size allowed them to boast they were the "biggest" paper in town.

Editors with overall responsibility for the paper have daily news conferences with subordinate editors. They can commit as much as an hour to mulling over what should run on the front page. A common fallacy is that they fret only about identifying the most important stories, which they will "play" most prominently. In reality the editors look for importance *and* diversity. Neither process is very scientific, which is why editors spend so much time at it.

Alf Goodykoontz, former executive editor of the Richmond *Times-Dispatch* in Virginia, identifies one of his greatest news mistakes as not giving sufficient prominence to Elvis Presley's death in 1977. It is easy to see why the editor might have thought the selection of a new director for the Federal Bureau of Investigation and the willingness of Soviet leader Leonid Brezhnev to negotiate with President Carter were more important that day. In retrospect, though, Elvis' death was obviously the big news. After all, most people today would be hard-pressed to remember who was selected as the FBI director, while many are still pondering the meaning—and truth—of Elvis' death.

To achieve diversity, editors avoid running only local, national, or international stories on the front page even if the biggest events of the day fall entirely in one category. Turning out a product that will interest everyone in their diverse audience, editors similarly look for fun-to-read feature stories even if those articles are not tied to breaking news.

Headline size is not a reliable yardstick of importance. An attractive page design depends on a variety of "head" sizes. Nor does the big news of the day always determine the front-page picture of the day. So much the better if the editors have a visually interesting photo with sharp color resolution to go with the main front-page story. But editors will often run a photograph that relates to a story inside the paper if the photo is superior and will enliven the page. Such a photo has the side benefit of tempting readers past the front page. In *USA Today*'s attempt to attract a diverse audience, it has a policy of placing a photo of at least one woman and one minority on the front page every day.

Influenced by *USA Today* and by television news, editors have begun to give more weight to stories with good visuals. New technologies have made it easier to dress up the paper with snappy graphics, and today's newspaper executives are afraid not to invest in the latest equipment at a time when they fear losing readers. The result is that newspapers use more color and enhanced visuals. In the old days a reporter might well take a camera along on a story, especially if he or she worked for a small paper. Reporters are now expected to come back not only with facts for a story that they can write but also with ideas that a graphic artist can convert into charts and tables that will run with the text.

Because they care so much about keeping the reader happy, newspapers have begun to favor shorter stories. People spend less time reading the newspaper these days, so they want stories in bite-size pieces. Also, they hate the hassle of rifling through the paper each time a story on page one "jumps" deep into an inside section.* *USA Today* believes in breaking potentially long stories into many smaller ones that can be grouped together.

One of the chief rules of newspaper design is that the paper should be predictable from day to day, with similar stories in the same place. This is called packaging. Newspapers have standard sections around different themes: national news, foreign news, sports news, business news, and so forth. The horoscope, the weather map, and the comics are supposed to appear in more or less the same spot each day. Other special news features also have homes in various parts of the paper. Every day, for instance, the Los Angeles *Times* runs a feature story in the left-hand column of the front page.

Special sections, like travel and food, come on the same day each week. Food sections often appear on Thursday because that's when supermarkets want to advertise. Travel sections appear on Sunday, a leisure day when readers are inclined to think about vacations. Theme considerations override newsworthiness. No matter how much big news occurs, the horoscope will be found in its usual place.

Many of the aggravations of reading a newspaper result from the limitations imposed by the physical dimensions of the paper. Continuation of stories to inside pages of the paper is necessary in order to get a broad sampling of stories on front pages. The only way to avoid jumping, as noted above, is to shorten stories.

---

* Ridding newspapers of jumps is not easy. The following appeared in the *Star-News* in Pasadena, California, in 1992: "We have made the commitment to our readers to minimize 'jumps,' those stories that continue from one page to another. Readers have told newspapers loud and often that they do not like such 'jumps,' and we've resolved to arrange our pages so that most stories will finish on the page they began." The problem was that to get the complete story on the design changes, the reader had to "jump" to another page.

History is partly to blame for lack of experimentation in newspaper size. Putting out those broadsheets required an enormous investment in equipment, which discouraged change and set the standard for newspapers.

The situation is similar to advances in typewriters. The original placement of keys in the old manual was designed to keep the typist from going too fast and jamming the machine. With electric typewriters and word processors, jamming is no longer a problem, but no one wants to learn a new, faster system, so keyboards have stayed the same. The result is that reporters type on traditional keyboards attached to high-powered computers, and you are reading newspapers of old-fashioned sizes even though they are printed on highly sophisticated presses that produce crisp color and fascinating graphics.

· · · · · · · · · · · · · · · · · · · · · · · · · · · · · · · · · · · · · · · · · · · · · · · · · · · · · · · · · · ·

### Aside: Devil's Glossary

Any venerable craft has its own peculiar insider language, and in the case of the press the lingo runs to the morbid and violent. Here is a sampling:

**Bleed.** An illustration that fills one or more outside margins, as in "the picture bled to the edge of the page."

**Blow up.** To make bigger, as in "blow up that guy" (in the photo).

**Body.** The main part of a news story.

**Boil.** To pare down and make a story more concise.

**Bullet.** A large dot, sometimes used to draw attention to each paragraph in a series that makes up a list.

**Bury.** To hide a phrase or fact inside the body of a story.

**Butcher.** To ruin a good story, as in "the editor butchered my copy."

**Cut.** To shorten a story; also, a newspaper illustration.

**Dead.** Text that has been thrown out or "killed."

**Deadline.** The final moment at which a news story has to be completed.

**Head shot.** A photo showing only the subject's head and neck.

**Hole.** Something that is missing in a story.

**Kill.** To throw out or withhold a story.*

---

*In the days of hot metal type, the receptacle for discarded type was called a "hell box," but it is seldom used today.

**Morgue.** The newspaper's library, which keeps clippings of old news stories in the event reporters wish to see what has been written before.*

**Pox.** Slang for "police."

**Slug.** An identifying word or phrase at the top of a story that is being continued on a second page.

**Tombstone.** To place two headlines side by side on the newspaper page.

**Widow.** A short line at the end of a paragraph; a widow is verboten if it is the first line to appear at the top of a newspaper, magazine, or book page.

..............................................................................

## Why Reporters Invert Pyramids

In the interest of appealing to as many readers as possible, most news stories are written for an audience with a ninth-grade reading ability.** The writing may not be poetry, but it still isn't easy. It demands skill and attention to a special set of rules.

The rule that journalism students hear the most is called the "inverted pyramid." For generations, this structure has governed the standard news story. To understand what it is, picture a triangle standing on one of its points instead of on its base. The reporter packs the most important details at the wide top of the story and the less important information below. Then the story can be shortened easily, if need be, with a swift chop off the bottom.

Like banner headlines and broadsheets, the inverted pyramid has a history. With the creation of the telegraph, reporters could send news long distances rapidly. The problem was the high cost of transmission and the possibility of interruptions in service. To take advantage of the new technology and minimize its pitfalls, editors discouraged long-winded, gilded prose that didn't get to the point right away. By avoiding narratives with a clear beginning, middle, and end, editors

---

* Morgues are becoming obsolete as a result of sophisticated electronic databases, which hold stories from many newspapers and thereby allow reporters to repeat not only their own errors but the errors of their competitors.

** It used to be eighth grade, says an expert who works on literacy projects using newspapers, but ninth grade now is about what eighth used to be.

also made it easier on themselves. They could fit a story into a finite space without a lot of work. In addition, giving the highlights of a news event right at the beginning of a story lends a sense of urgency befitting a newspaper—especially one competing for the attention of busy readers. Unlike a poem or a short piece of fiction, the reader is not forced to read to the end to get the meaning.

Reconfiguring reality into this format is not as easy as it sounds. Imagine yourself as a reporter covering a four-hour school board meeting with a twelve-item agenda. When the meeting concludes, you have about thirty minutes before deadline to write—or phone in—350 words on what happened. While musing over the myriad choices, you are mindful that everything the public is to learn about that school board meeting is in your sweaty hands—and those of your competitor.

The method of handling this particular story really boils down to one of two classic approaches: As noted in an earlier section, the summary lead tries to capture the essence of the event; the single-shot lead takes aim at the most newsworthy item—or the one you think is most newsworthy.* Then, you have to decide what to write next. Do you elaborate on what was said in the lead, or do you move on to new information? At what point do you leaven the story with a good quote or "color"? How much background is needed to explain the context? What information do you leave out?

While all these involve judgment calls, journalists have some clear guidelines. As mentioned earlier, one of them is to answer the Who, What, Where, When, Why, and How. This is the immutable journalistic law of the Five *W*s and *H*. Journalists also know that good news writing shows rather than tells, and that it is devoid of judgmental adjectives, obtuse jargon, and complicated clauses. The story should be enticing without sacrificing accuracy, substance, balance, taste, context, tone, relevance, or timeliness. And preferably by the deadline in thirty minutes, thank you.

Rules for clear writing have varied from era to era, but research has shown that simple words and short, direct sentences are the easiest to read. Rudolf Flesch, an Austrian-born etymologist who became a pioneer in the study of modern English readability in the 1940s and 1950s, even developed a formula for news writing that recommended

---

* *Lead* has two meanings in journalism: similar to a sales person's lead, a prospect to pursue, or the first paragraph in a story.

keeping sentences to 17 words or less. Today, you more often see sentences running 100 words and less allegiance to the summary lead.

This change is part of a larger transformation of news writing. The "hard news" story (as opposed to a feature or analysis piece) is more flexible today than it used to be. For one thing competition from television, which can provide news seconds after it happens, has diminished the importance of urgency in print stories. Computers make it easier to write stories to length rather than simply lopping off the end to make it fit (something printers often did without even consulting editors). Finally, editors are looking for more engaging writing in hopes they can stanch the decline in readers.

As a result, more newspapers hire writing coaches, and reporters concentrate more on context and storytelling than they did in the past. Not long ago, the lead story in the New York *Times* was hard, breaking news, period. Today you can find a main story like this one from March 27, 1995, describing a trend: "With a speed so rapid that many medical experts are taken aback, genetic tests that can tell if a person is likely to get cancer are entering the marketplace."

Experimenting with other approaches besides the old upside-down triangle, writing coaches talk in terms of the "champagne glass" style. This variation puts the important information in the top and the supporting material in the middle stem. And ideally the base will have a snappy conclusion, "a reward to the reader," says longtime editor Richard Dudman.

But when it comes to succinctly delivering the fundamental facts, no one has yet found a better model than that old inverted pyramid. Many editors who are trying to get better writing in the paper worry that straying from conventions will encourage young reporters to concentrate on being the next Hemingway at the expense of getting the facts.

There's a popular saw in the news business that "a good story writes itself." The implication is that the information is so compelling, you don't really have to think about how you present it. The AP's first bulletin on the shooting of Lincoln was "The president was shot in a theatre tonight and is perhaps mortally wounded." Such hard leads continue to work today for breaking stories.* But what if you have to

---

* The lead Washington *Post* story on the attempted assassination of President Reagan in 1981 began: "President Reagan survived an assassination attempt yesterday when a revolver-wielding gunman waiting among reporters

write a thoughtful piece about the first landing on the moon? That can paralyze the most experienced pro.

"To write well is as difficult as being good," wrote Somerset Maugham. Some journalists have great literary virtue. Occasionally, they even write poetry.*

## Why Granny's Obituary Didn't Make the Morning Edition

Let's get one thing straight right now: It had nothing to do with Granny. Of course, if she had been really famous . . . But that's another issue.

In this case, the journalist is probably more your ally than your nemesis. The editor wanted your grandmother's obituary to appear in the paper almost as much as you did. The villain here was space—or the lack of it. In newspaper terms it is called the "news hole," the space allocated in the daily paper for news as opposed to advertisements.**

The news hole is one of the fundamental realities of newspaper life. Editors grudgingly live by it. Reporters disdain it. The reason is that it is largely out of their control. The size of a news hole is dictated by the volume of advertising scheduled for a given newspaper edition. If the number of ad inches happens to be large on a particular day, the space for news is proportionately higher, and vice versa.

---

and photographers on the sidewalk outside the Washington Hilton hotel fired a bullet into his chest." This is a time-honored approach, but newspapers today also give much more space to thoughtful background pieces that don't use the inverted pyramid style. Television conditions many of these stories. Here is a page-six report from the New York *Times:* "Videotapes of the attempted assassination of President Reagan began running on the three major television networks less than half an hour after the shooting at the Washington Hilton Hotel yesterday. What ensued was a graphic documentation, from a variety of camera angles, of the attempt on the President's life."

\* To great gasps from his journalistic brethren, *Time* reporter Strobe Talbot once wrote a poem published in the *New Yorker.* Showing just how broad-based he was, Talbot went on to be deputy secretary of state in the Clinton administration.

\*\* The term used to describe the amount of advertising is *linage.*

This is how the space system typically works at a daily morning newspaper (that is, one that goes to press in the late evening and lands on your doorstep before breakfast):

Every day at about 11 A.M., the advertising department sends to the editor a set of "dummy" sheets that shows the ads already blocked out for the next day's paper. The editor will make a quick calculation and come up with a number—say, 1,020—for the number of column inches making up the day's news hole.

Each section of the paper—national and international news, local news, sports, lifestyle—is assigned its own news hole. The "metro" (city) section of the newspaper may have a small news hole because there are few local ads. But the section dealing with national news may have a windfall of space that day because an airline decided to announce its new fares to the Caribbean. Advertisers have their favorite sections. A local hardware store may not want to have its ad appear in the international section because it thinks that section won't get a lot of tool-buying readers.

Only a handful of people in the newsroom know the size of the news hole set for the day. Reporters don't pay much attention. They receive their assignments and then get on with writing them. Their goal is to try hard to get their own story into tomorrow's paper; someone else's story can be sacrificed. Editors, meanwhile, are thinking something like: "How can I stuff a twenty-inch story into a ten-inch hole?"

Very few parts of a newspaper are insulated from these vicissitudes of the marketplace, but the front page is usually one of them. In most papers no ads are allowed on page one. Sometimes front-page space is allocated for a very small classified announcement, but newsroom purists wrinkle their noses at such intrusions.

While the front page is sacred, the news operation side often feels abused by the vagaries of advertising decisions on the inside pages. In particular, the size of the news hole can change during the course of the day, sometimes wildly. A newspaper generally has an even number of pages because it must fill both sides of each page of newsprint (the actual pulp paper comes in giant rolls and is cut after it comes off the presses). If an ad takes up one whole side of a page, the other side has to be filled with something. An editor who had too much news for the paper may now find there isn't enough. In such a case, the editor turns to a drawer (now a computer) for that "soft" and timeless feature story waiting to see the light of day.

The converse can happen, too. That full-page ad can be dropped and the whole other side of the page, once planned for news, disappears, or more ads can come in, thus reducing the space for news. The reaction is summed up in Jane Harrigan's day-in-a-life study of a daily newspaper: "On a night when the news hole is tight, a copy editor will curse advertising's dominance as she trims yet another inch from a story whose author, she knows, will spew coffee in a rage when he sees the paper in the morning."

Shrinking news holes are more common than expanding ones. That is an immutable law of the American press, and that is what happened to Granny's obit.

## Why Journalists Do "Thumb-Suckers"

Newspapers have an anatomy. Like the organs of the human body, various types of stories perform different functions while working together. Some are vital organs, and some are appendices to the paper's mission.

*Hard news* is the heart of the newspaper, what happened in the last twenty-four hours: A two-car crash killed six on Highway 10; Mayor Latham announced that GE would build a new plant in Pickerington; the Dow Jones industrial average rose ten points in heavy trading.

As explained in previous chapters, the hard-news formula does not relieve journalists of the chore of making choices. They must organize information around what they deem to be the most newsworthy theme; they build the story from a jumble of data and quotes. Although much judgment goes into hard-news reporting, clear limits are imposed on the journalist. Who, what, where, and when get a lot more attention than why and how.

To get at those two more elusive aspects of the news, journalists do what they jokingly call the "thumb-sucker." This is a story that explains the significance of the news. It, too, is found in the news sections of the paper and is written by the same reporters who cover hard news. Virtually every good newspaper is so jealous of its credibility as a source of objective news that it labels these stories *news analysis* so they will not be confused with hard news. Even so, the goal here is not to provide the reporter's opinion of the news but to put the news into context.

*Features* are sometimes labeled, sometimes not. Either way the intent is to give a human-interest angle. Often features relate to the news, for instance, the agony of wives waiting for their husbands to be dug out of a collapsed mine shaft. But features can also be done for their own sake. The fireman-rescues-the-cat-from-the-tree story is in this genre. Features use humor and pathos.

Signed *columns* appear throughout the paper and typically present a person's opinion. In this category you find movie reviews, political commentary, and investment advice. But the chief place for out-and-out opinion is the editorial page and the op-ed page, as the opposite-editorial page of commentary is called.

While hard news, news analysis, and features are written by reporters in various sections of the newspaper, a separate staff writes *editorials.* On large papers editorial writers meet as an editorial board to decide the newspaper's position on an issue or event. In some newspapers, the editor heads the editorial board; in others the publisher does. Either way, a sharp distinction exists between editorials and what appears on news pages.

A classic example of this division is the *Wall Street Journal.* Its editorial page shows a pronounced conservative point of view, while its news pages contain stories often unfavorable toward business and positive about liberal causes. During the investigation of President Clinton by special counsel Robert B. Fiske, Jr., a *Journal* news headline read: "Fiske Gets Off to Fast Start in Whitewater Probe by Moving Forward Aggressively on All Fronts." Said the headline on the editorial page: "The Fiske Cover-Up II." In the words of the *Journal's* Washington bureau chief, "There is this tradition of not just separation but competition—or enmity."

Editorials are not signed. They are presented as the newspaper's opinion. The op-ed page, an invention years ago of the long defunct New York *World,* carries signed opinions. Sometimes these come from a reporter on the newspaper. David Broder of the Washington *Post* is a reporter *and* a columnist. More often, though, those who write on the op-ed page are either full-time columnists whose trade is opinion or they are members of the public, usually experts, who have something to say. Some metropolitan newspapers can receive as many as two hundred op-ed submissions a day from people who want

## Aside: The Organization of a Newspaper

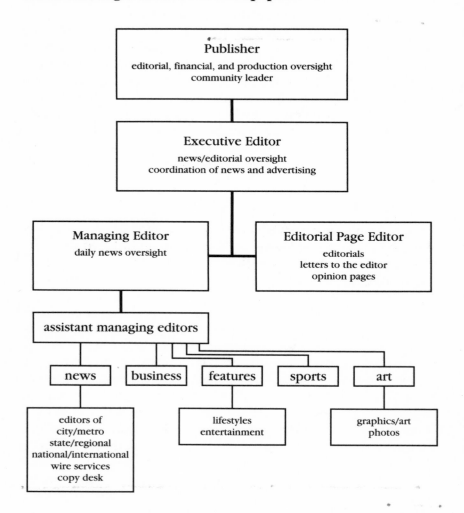

This chart shows a typical editorial management structure of a newspaper with a circulation of 50,000 to 100,000. The structure varies depending on the newspaper's size. At smaller papers the publisher is more involved with the daily operations and oversees the editorial page.

to get something off their chests. Most papers can use only one or two. Typically newspapers try to run a variety of commentators on their opinion page. Even in opinion they strive for balance.

A single news event can lead to every type of story mentioned above. The hard news story might be that Congress voted down a tax increase. A news analysis story might explain that election-year political concerns shaped the outcome. The news feature might look at the soul-searching of one legislator who wanted to vote yes but was afraid of voter repercussion. The editorial page might chide Congress for lack of courage while columnists George Will (a conservative) and William Raspberry (a liberal) voice opposing views on the op-ed page.

## Why Headlines Squeeze the Truth

When readers complain about a newspaper story, they often are referring to the headline, not what's below it. Reporters know the problem well. They, too, complain when editors derail a story with a head that is misleading or inaccurate.

Reporters don't write headlines except at the smallest newspapers. "Heads" are composed by copy editors, portrayed in black-and-white movies wearing eyeshades and sleeve garters, bent over their paper-strewn desks with a perpetual frown on their shadowed faces.

Having these specialists write heads should make for more accuracy, not less. So what's the problem? Is the copy desk, where they work, a journalistic backwater where editors put those who can't be trusted with the real work of reporting?

As easy as it is to call copy editors feckless, it's the task itself that causes the problems. A headline writer has to cram the meaning of a story into a handful of words, and this must be accomplished with accuracy and, if possible, zip. Often this has to be done very quickly (since reporters are notoriously late in meeting their copy deadlines). Like those who build ships in bottles, headline writers must work magic in tiny spaces.

When done well, headline writing is often taken for granted. When done badly, it spawns anger, ridicule, or outright hilarity. "Coach Sells Wife on Move to Dayton" is an example of what can go wrong. Once in a while, however, a headline is so good it becomes as memorable as a good news story. President Ford's refusal in 1975 to give financial aid to New York City led to this celebrated example in the *Daily News:* "Ford to City: Drop Dead." Another classic appeared in the show-business newspaper *Variety* over a 1935 story saying that farm communities didn't pay to see movies about themselves: "Sticks Nix Hicks Pix."

Headlines have several purposes: to summarize a story, to draw attention to a story, and to indicate how the paper views the story's importance. To accomplish this, a number of variables are brought into the decision-making process, among them the size of the letters, the width and depth of the headline, and sometimes the typeface.

These days, the job is made easier by the computer, which does the space measuring and helps find synonyms and the like. But it hasn't yet replaced the fertile mind when it comes to capturing the essence of a story with verve and clarity. And computers can't keep copy editors from writing themselves into awkward corners.

The ambiguity of our language provides one of the biggest traps, such as the "two-faced" head: "Mayor Gets Girl's Calf" . . . "Alabama Bars Financing Gay Groups" . . . "Man Freed in Businessman's Suit" . . . or "Reporter Finishes Sentence." (Just joking, folks.) Of course, double meanings can also create opportunities: "Nudes Pinched in Art Gallery Theft" . . . "Man Held in Stolen Watch Case."

Then there's the problem of switching nouns and verbs with adjectives: "President Gives Poor Advice on Jobs" . . . "Candidate Arrested at Rally for Striking Workers." Clumsy juxtaposition offers another kind of problem: "Aid Sought for Every Child by President" . . . "Woman Dies Defending Gift from Muggers."

Sometimes the poor copy editor is blindsided by fate itself. The *Arizona Republic* once ran a story called "Sexually Aggressive Teen-Age Girls." It appeared next to an advertisement entitled "Best Gifts for Men."

A "typo" or misspelling can mean disaster: "Judge Rapes Defense Attorney in Assault Case." These headline errors (one can only assume they are inadvertent) are the bane of newspapers because they are so obvious—and memorable. One still recalled by old-timers was the headline in the Washington *Post* reporting that President Franklin Roosevelt had to cancel a press conference because he was down with a cold: "FDR in Bed with Coed."

Newspapers have not always striven for compelling headlines. Before newspapers became a truly mass medium in the mid-nineteenth century, heads were used merely to organize information on the page: "Latest News from the Front." Half the column would be eaten up in subheads summarizing information in the story. Competition among papers helped fuel the drive for sensational headlines, such as an 1870s humdinger in a Chicago *Times* story about the hanging of four murderers: "Jerked to Jesus."

The age of big, bold, brassy headlines is now dying largely because the need to catch a reader's eye at the newsstand has been replaced by the guaranteed subscription at home. Now the emphasis is more on the total page design and packaging of news, with the headline relegated to a lesser role.

Still, headline writers must be as skilled as ever. Like aficionados of crossword puzzles, they must have a repertoire of short, meaningful words. They must be wary of making a mistake that can lead to a libel suit. They must add to the story, not take away from it. Headline writers, for instance, often repeat a key phrase from the story. But if a story ends with a good punchline, the headline isn't supposed to give it away.

## Why Newspapers Look Alike

If you were to lay out on a table most of the nation's daily newspapers, you would notice a remarkable similarity not only in their design and form but also in content. Hardly remarkable, you might say, given the fact they are all the same product, just different brand names. But this is an industry peopled by reporters and editors who pride themselves on independence.

One of the more obvious points of similarity is the diet of national and international stories on the front pages. Most local news organizations cannot afford bureaus even in their own state capitals, much less in Washington or overseas. So they rely on the news agencies (often called "wire services" or just "wires") for information from outside their immediate area.

Of course, that doesn't explain a similar phenomenon at the largest newspapers, which have their own far-flung networks of correspondents. Although the New York *Times,* Los Angeles *Times,* Chicago *Tribune,* Miami *Herald,* and Washington *Post* may differ some, the themes on international and national stories are similar as well. Whether it be Bosnia, Rwanda, North Korea, or health care reform, everyone seems to be covering the same stuff.

In 1792 Congress gave each newspaper the right to send one copy postage-free to all its cousins. The idea was to help newspapers learn from one another. Journalists haven't needed much coaxing when it comes to looking over each other's shoulders. Editors read other newspapers to ensure they aren't missing anything, and reporters build on each other's stories, something made easier by computerized databases that store stories from many papers and allow virtually instant recall. Contradictory though it may seem, fiercely competitive journalists herd together when covering events, not because they are afraid of outsiders but because they don't want to miss a story that others may get.

One of the leading political journalists in America is Associated Press writer Walter Mears. Mears earned his reputation not only by being one of the fastest writers in the business but by having an uncanny knack for quickly grasping the essence of a breaking political story. Because of this knack, his colleagues during presidential campaigns took cues from him. As documented by Timothy Crouse in *The Boys on the Bus,* he became known on the campaign trail as "What's-the-Lead-Walter." His exploits during the 1976 Carter campaign won Mears a Pulitzer Prize.

One reason Mears was so central to this phenomenon was his vantage point as a news agency writer. Every correspondent on that campaign bus knew perfectly well that his editor back home was reading Mears's rapid-fire "leads" off the AP wire. If the newspaper's own reporter didn't have the same angle on the story as the one on the wire, he risked getting a "callback" (sometimes called a "rocket") from the editor: "Mears has such-and-such. Where's ours?" Reporters really hate rockets. Thus, it behooved the boys on the bus to ask before filing their stories, "What's the lead, Walter?"

One of the other powerful influences on news conformity, unseen by the general public, is the digest of "top stories" filed to newspapers and stations every couple of hours by the news agencies. An editor who ignores the digest does so at his or her peril, because it tends to set the agenda for what the nation's media regard as important.

Another factor that contributes to homogeneity is chain ownership. When a chain buys a locally owned newspaper, it quite often improves the newspaper's quality, noted Nashville *Tennessean* publisher

John Seigenthaler in 1979, shortly before Gannett bought the paper. But, he added, "As I read over Gannett papers in the chain it does seem to me that there is a sameness about them." Gannett develops news and layout formulas it expects all of its papers to follow. Editors meet at Gannett headquarters regularly to critique each other's product, a group-think process that reinforces the inclination to conform.

Finally, there is the all-important matter of consensus on news values. Despite each newspaper, magazine, radio station, and television station calling its own shots, journalists generally agree on what's a hot story, what's a "snore," and what's bogus. They may not be able to explain why; they just know. News values are part of the institutional memory.

The vast network of journalism schools in America helps maintain this memory, as does the newsroom practice of passing on the myth and legend of the business. Journalists parrot the same old slogans, perhaps the most famous being one from an editor of the New York *Sun* more than a century ago: "When a dog bites a man, that is *not* news, but when a man bites a dog, that is news."

Thus even local news pages in one community look roughly like local news pages in another: a crime or car accident, a new board of education budget, a report on downtown traffic hazards, a rezoning controversy.

Notwithstanding the suspicions of conspiracy theorists, the nation's editors are not putting their heads together each day to decide what should be on the front page. But they *are* reading the same wires and the syndicates. They are watching the same news programs on CNN and the networks. They are reading their major competitors or at least keeping track of what they cover—and how they cover it. (Consider the *USA Today* invention of the color weather map, which is now in widespread use.) They are attending the same media conventions where discussion typically turns to ideas for attracting and keeping readers. Competitive or not, one gets a certain amount of strength and comfort from conformity.

# IV

## What's News and What's Not

# Why the Status Quo Is Not News

"A duplex on Oak Street burned to the ground yesterday . . ."

"The president unveiled a plan to curb federal spending . . ."

"The National Weather Service today predicted 15 inches of snow across the Midwest by late Tuesday . . ."

When a dog bites a man, as the New York *Sun* editor said, it isn't news. But when a man bites a dog, it is. The principle enshrined in this aphorism is that the status quo—the expected, the routine—is generally not newsworthy. Readers don't want long stories telling them nothing has changed in the last day or so. They plunk down fifty cents for a newpaper and expect to find out what's *new*. To meet this need, journalists think chiefly in terms of what is called breaking news—changes from the normal occurring right now. It may be interesting that a man bit a dog ten years ago, but it isn't newsworthy.

The three stories above are typical. The Oak Street fire story is a clear-cut news event. A house has been reduced to ashes. Period. The presidential plan is news because the president just introduced it. It will lead to more news when in the next twenty-four hours political leaders on both sides give the press their reactions. The National Weather Service story is attractive not only because it is timely and of vital interest but also because it has real numbers—fifteen inches of snow. Reporters love statistics. Here is *precise* change.

But if you are getting lots of news when you pick up a newspaper, you need to remember what you aren't getting. Pressed up close to events, journalists often lack perspective. In the rush to tell you what is different, they don't dwell on what has stayed the same.

In most cases this presents no problem. You supply the perspective. After reading a story about that Oak Street home burning to the

ground, you don't think that all homes in your community are reduced to ashes. Likewise, you know that the president's spending
plan is one of many over the years; depending on your view of the
president, you're either skeptical or are upbeat about its success. You
know that heavy snow is common in the Midwest, so fifteen inches
more or less is not going to make you pack your bags; you'd be much
more worried if Alabama were to be buried in snow.

But when you don't know the context, you may draw the wrong
conclusion. As an example, consider the steady stream of stories about
crime in cities like Washington or New York. If you don't live there,
you may have an exaggerated picture of the dangers and have forgotten that most residents walk the streets without fear. Recall how for-
eigners regarded Chicago in the 1920s. News stories of the time created the image of a city beset by machine gun–toting gangsters.

The same problem occurs with news on health studies. One year
the newspaper reports that butter isn't good for you; the next year
you learn that butter is okay, but margarine isn't. One month the
newspaper carries a report from the Centers for Disease Control saying any exercise will prolong your life; the following month comes
the story of a Harvard University study finding that only people who
exercised regularly and strenuously lived longer. The rhythm of science and the rhythm of journalism are as different as the waltz and
the flamenco. Medical experts and scientists see each health study as
an inconclusive piece of information in a larger mosaic that takes
shape over many years. The newspaper concentrates on today's study,
not what remains as inconclusive as it was yesterday (*i.e.*, on what is
not news). The result is quite unhealthy, for it encourages frustrated
readers to throw up their hands and say, "Nothing is good for you, so
why should I change my lifestyle?"

A case study of emphasizing change at the expense of continuity
came in 1984 when the Communist Chinese announced a series of
economic reforms. Reports on the new economic program ran on
many front pages with leads like this one in the New York *Times:*
"China announced plans today for sweeping changes in its urban
economy that will introduce capitalist-style market forces and reduce
government control." Emphasizing what was new in the announced
program, the *Times* story said almost nothing about what was the
same—and what it did say about that was presented as an after-
thought. In the seventh paragraph it noted that diplomats believed

the reforms "would accelerate China's repudiation of the rigid system of central planning and economic control borrowed by Mao Zedong from the Soviet Union, but would not repudiate Communism itself." The average reader, plowing through the paper and having little personal experience with China, would be excused for thinking China was about to be utterly transformed into a free-market system.*

All of which proves that journalists, who are said to write the first draft of history, emphasize what's new. The reader must remember to think about what's staying the same.

· · · · · · · · · · · · · · · · · · · · · · · · · · · · · · · · · · · · · · · · · · · · · · · · · · · · · · · · · · · · · · · ·

## Aside: You Can't Count on Statistics

"The government are very keen on amassing statistics," said Sir Josiah Stamp, a British official at the turn of the century. "They collect them, add them, raise them to the *n*th power, take the cube root and prepare wonderful diagrams. But you must never forget that every one of these figures comes in the first instance from the village watchman, who just puts down what he damn pleases."

Statistics are reassuring. They look so exact, so scientific. "Reporters and editors, sensitive to accusations of bias, appreciate the apparent neutrality of numbers," says *Wall Street Journal* reporter and editor Cynthia Crossen. But, as Crossen notes, numbers are not neutral. Studies can be flawed, sometimes purposely by special interest groups who conduct them, sometimes inadvertently by neutral but fallible researchers. The most expertly done studies are subject to error. Unfortunately, space constraints (and ignorance) often prevent journalists from providing the warnings that a reputable polling firm

---

\* In the coming months news stories continued to emphasize change rather than continuity. Xinhua, the Chinese government-run news agency, distributed a picture of the first Chinese family to own a car. The real story, of course, was that every other family in the country did not own a car. But American picture editors could not resist publishing that shot—nor the Xinhua picture that appeared a few days later of the first family to own an airplane.

The press finally caught up with reality. A reporter went out to interview the family with the plane and found that they did not own it at all. But news of that charade was not nearly as prominent as the front-page stories that had come before.

would include in its own report. Here, for instance, is language from a Louis Harris study of Americans' efforts to promote good health:

> Even the best designed surveys are liable to several possible sources of error. The most important are:
>     • *Nonresponse* (if those who are interviewed differ from those who are not interviewed). [For example, you may not have interviewed the right categories of people.]
>     • *Random or sampling error,* which may in theory be substantial, even on very large surveys. Contrary to the impression given by the typical media caveat, there is no way to calculate the maximum possible error for any survey. All we deal in are probabilities.
>     • *Question wording,* particularly where the survey is measuring an attitude or a future intention and not a "fact." Several equally good questions may yield several different (and equally valid) responses. In addition, question sequence can influence the responses, particularly to attitude questions.

. . . . . . . . . . . . . . . . . . . . . . . . . . . . . . . . . . . . . . . . . . . . . . . . . . . . . . . . . . . . . . . . . . . . . . . . . . . . . . . . .

# Why No News Is Good News

Letter to the Editor:
What a newspaper! News—of what? Killings, accidents, rape . . . teenagers in trouble. But—have a group of kids spend a Sunday afternoon driving around Lake Harriet in a gaily decorated 1926 Ford open air car and afterwards entertain the adults at a GOP rally with their band and guitars and songs—not a word, morning or evening.

Mark Twain would have appreciated this letter to the editor of a Minneapolis newspaper in the 1960s. Although once a journalist himself, Twain confessed that the news he read in the morning paper was depressing enough to "cause me to put in the rest of the day pleading for the damnation of the human race."

To this day Americans put up with an awful lot of bad news. And they get sick of it. Virtually by definition, the news seems to be negative. No news, it would seem, is good news.

Journalists tend to be defensive on this subject. One of the common comebacks is that the news isn't always bad. They point to all the good-news events that make the paper, like the return of a missing child or the retiring mailman who is feted by a grateful community. In addition, they note, good news often results from the bad.

Government corruption is uncovered, and the rascals are thrown out of office; coverage of that gruesome car crash leads to a traffic light at a dangerous intersection; graphic photographs of starving children in Somalia prompt more foreign aid.

Pollster George Gallup, who has read America's pulse for more than forty years, is not persuaded. Journalists, he thinks, are preoccupied with negative news at the expense of balanced reality. And he can draw on plenty of evidence to show that the public feels that way. What may be more interesting, though, is not whether one side is wrong and the other right but the intensity with which each side holds to its point of view.

A 1993 survey by the Freedom Forum First Amendment Center found strikingly divergent sentiment. "Journalists by their nature report the bad news and ignore the good, no matter how well things are going in America, say 60 percent of the politicians and 53 percent of the public. 'Do not!' respond 76 percent of journalists." The Times Mirror Center for the People and the Press reported a similar finding in 1995. Two-thirds of the public and even more opinion leaders believe the press concentrates too much on misdeeds. Only 30 percent of the national newspaper journalists and 14 percent of their local counterparts feel that way.

Some tough-minded journalists do worry about negativism. "There's too much cynicism out there, and it's like a snake swallowing its tail," says Thomas Winship, retired editor of the Boston *Globe*. "The public gets cynical about Congress, largely because the press is so cynical about Congress." Says Eileen Shanahan, Washington bureau chief for the St. Petersburg *Times,* "We in journalism . . . seldom cover anything but the failures, fostering in our readers and viewers the conviction there is no hope—no point in even trying to fix any of the things that are so terribly wrong in our country, or even improve them a little."

Capitalizing on this concern, Al Neuharth founded the newspaper *USA Today* in 1982 on what he called "the journalism of hope, rather than the journalism of despair." He said Americans were tired of having their world portrayed with such darkness. Although Neuharth retired as Gannett chairman in 1990, the newspaper continues to have an upbeat approach to news. Critics disdain this as simply the flip side of an equally unreal world: Pollyanna instead of Frankenstein. Journalists are sensitive about such criticism: A former *USA Today* editor gets defensive when that daily is called "a happy paper" and will gladly point out all the bad news it carries.

This sensitivity is revealing. The problem of negativism has much to do with expectations the press has of itself. Journalists work in a culture that respects toughness. Significantly, the Times Mirror survey found that 80 percent of the national print journalists and 70 percent of those at the local level thought their publications were more concerned about being too soft than about being too hard on the people they cover. "The hardest thing in the world is to write an admiring piece," says *New Republic* columnist Michael Kinsley. "It's much easier to do a hatchet job." Those 100 percent sweet profiles make a journalist look like a toady, the surest way to be ridiculed by news colleagues.

Recall also the previous section. The bedrock criterion for what constitutes news in the American press is change, and change begets trauma. And trauma is usually unpleasant. If the plane lands on time (instead of crashing) or if the teachers go to class (instead of striking), there is nothing to report. The bizarre and violent have been the stuff of news since the press in America became a mass medium.

Another factor is the press's self-appointed role as the public's "watchdog," always on the lookout for trouble. The industry mind-set assumes that somewhere, somehow, the public is being cheated. Of course, the government helps. Whether cheating or not, it fosters an atmosphere of negativity by *its* attitude. It is supposed to tackle problems, and the press is there to chronicle them.

The search for easy-to-report factual news lends itself to crime and accidents. Such news was not even considered newsworthy until the penny press came along. But when it did, murders and burning houses offered an ideal way to attract readers, avoid partisan political battles, stick to the facts—and do so without large expenses for reporters. While the lurid crime stories offered by the penny press are now considered bad form, the continued practice of assigning reporters to cover the police and court systems guarantees a plethora of bad news. These places are devoted to tragedy and unpleasantness.

Finally, journalists tend to preoccupy themselves with the search for dragons. Since childhood we have been accustomed to stories with heroes and villains, and the news industry has kept this expectation alive. The clash of titans is the stuff not only of sports coverage but political reporting as well. Clashes do not normally fall under the definition of "good news" and often produce *ad hominem* attacks during political campaigns, which become news.

In answering critics, journalists often avoid discussing the complexities. Much easier to offer pat answers. News is news, they say, and it's not their job to weigh the day's coverage based on whether it is uplifting. This, they also say, would prompt a dangerous form of self-censorship and cast the journalist in the role of chamber of commerce. The press did not invent tax fraud, elect that corrupt official, burn down that house, mug that jogger, or suppress that embarrassing report. "Don't shoot the messenger for the message."

The ultimate rejoinder, of course, relates more to the newspaper reader than to the newspaper reporter. The proof of news, editors contend, can be found in audience reaction—what people prefer to read, view, and hear from their media. People may say they dislike bad news, but they also have a voracious appetite for what Twain called the "depravities and baseness and hypocrisies and cruelties that make up civilization."

## Why You Read So Much About Government

On a random Tuesday in the fall of 1992, five of the seven stories on the front page of the New York *Times* were about government. The other two, reporting an earthquake in Egypt and the rise of tuberculosis in the United States, relied heavily on government sources. In the southern part of the United States, six of the Baton Rouge *Advocate*'s eight front-page stories were devoted to politics and government, ranging from plans for a new airport to presidential debates. The other two stories, on the earthquake and a Chinese Communist party congress, drew on government sources.

One conclusion that might be reached about these stories is that the press is relentless in seeking out information about government. But there is another explanation for the vast amounts of government news. It is easy to get. In theory and in practice, our government is organized to be accessible.

"The basis of our government being the opinion of the people, the very first object should be to keep that right; and were it left to me to decide whether we should have a government without newspapers, or newspapers without a government, I should not hesitate a moment to prefer the latter," Jefferson once said, summing up a common opinion among our nation's Founders. Behind this sentiment is the deepseated American suspicion of government. Leaders like Jefferson, who chafed at the idea that kings were immune from criticism, wanted checks against leaders who might try to arrogate too much power to themselves. A relatively unrestrained press, like an independent Congress and judiciary, was a step in that direction.

The British had something of the same idea themselves: Edmund Burke supposedly was the first to talk about the press as the Fourth Estate.* But American revolutionaries were willing to have the press go further than the British dared to let them tread, a situation that remains today despite many similarities between the two systems.

This is not to deny that our own government prefers to avoid unpleasant scrutiny and, in hopes of achieving that, throws up barriers to critical coverage. This not only happens but it is more the rule than the exception. Jefferson himself thoroughly disliked much of the coverage he received and wondered whether the press should, after all, be restrained. At one point he suggested to a confederate that "a few prosecutions of the most eminent offenders would have a wholesome effect in restoring the integrity of the presses." But the weight of American tradition favors the journalist.

In the United States system, there is no government-owned newspaper. The Congress is so concerned about the executive branch sending out self-aggrandizing propaganda that it will not allow publications printed by the U.S. Information Agency to be distributed in the United States. Those publications can only be distributed abroad. If government officials or political leaders want to get information to the American public, they must compete for media attention just like anyone else. And like everyone else wanting attention, political leaders and government bureaucrats create vast pools of information and news that they pipe to the media.

In 1993, the federal government employed 4,438 public affairs specialists and 1,940 writer-editors—according to a public affairs special-

---

* In feudal times the three estates were the Lords Spiritual (clergy), the Lords Temporal (nobility), and the Commons (knights and burgesses). According to Thomas Carlyle, Burke said, "There are three estates in Parliament but in the Reporters' Gallery yonder there sits a Fourth Estate more important far than they all." But the original source of the term may have been William Cobbitt, an early nineteenth-century British journalist.

ist with the U.S. Office of Personnel Management. And that left untold others whose job it was to handle the care and feeding of journalists. The National Aeronautics and Space Agency (NASA) fares so well in winning hefty government appropriations largely because its high-powered public relations activities have built favorable public support. For their part, each senator and representative on Capitol Hill has press aides who can use liberally subsidized postage rates to mail out news releases and in-house television and radio studios to prepare materials for media.

Speaking of Washington, D.C., the renegade journalist I. F. Stone once noted that there is "no other city, and no other world capital, in which life is made so easy for the newspaperman." But Washington is not the only locale with a government that caters to reporters. The city police department and mayor have their press aides as well. So do governors and the folks in state legislatures.

One branch of government does not have elections and worries little about government appropriations: the federal judiciary. It is also the least well covered. Supreme Court nominations get attention. But after being confirmed, justices remain remarkably out of the lime-light.

Accustomed to access, the press confidently demands the government open meetings and files. The Freedom of Information Act is as American as an ornery press. Under FOIA, passed in 1967, the government must, with some exceptions, make available to anyone requesting them records, documents, forms, and proceedings that are in the public interest. Journalists are typically in the front ranks of those wielding FOIA laws, often with fruitful results. Meanwhile, laws at the local level, also promoted by the media, guarantee that government gatherings will be open to the public. Use of the term *sunshine laws* to describe this legislation suggests how healthy open meetings are regarded in the United States.

A prime example of the ease with which reporters can get even explosive information about government activity was a Kansas City *Times* exposé on foreign aid during the Carter administration. The series elaborated a litany of failed projects and corrupt aid officials. The results seemed to be in the best tradition of tough investigative reporting of government. Here was a federal agency wasting taxpayers' money. But the discriminating reader would have realized something else, which the reporter played down. The prime source for this series of articles was none other than the government agency being criticized. The Agency for International Development had created an internal staff of auditors and investigators who produced endless reports. A reporter could expose the foreign aid program without even going overseas. All the journalist needed to do was sit in the agency's library and plow through its files.

The public can take comfort in reporters getting such easy access to government news. But easy access can also lure journalists away from stories. Politicians have learned that the way to tame the most energetic journalists is to feed them information at such a voluminous rate that they don't have time to sniff around for offbeat news. The White House press corps is a captive audience. When the president travels, the White House staff lays on an extra plane for the press. When the president is at home, the White House press corps sits around waiting for news releases or other announcements to be issued from the press secretary's office a few feet away. Reporters dare not take their eyes off the daily fare lest they miss a big story and incur the wrath of their editor.

A kind of irony is at work in this American tradition of government access. In a society where government is supposed to be small and private initiative large, it might be expected that more newsworthy activity would take place outside politics. Yet the private sector remained a black hole of news until recently, and the press still has a long way to go before business pages do their jobs fully. Similarly, philanthropy and charity are private activities in the United States, in contrast to Europe where such functions are regarded as the job of government and political parties. Yet, again, the press has given scant attention to nonprofit organizations.

But business and charity are not grouped in capitals or city halls. They are not constitutionally accountable to the people. Their leaders are not subject to public election. And so they are harder to cover.

The most extreme example of difficult news to cover, however, is foreign news. It may be more important than ever, but it's hard to find in your paper, as the next section explains.

## Why One Englishman Equals Ten Frenchmen

A British press baron once posted this notice in his newsroom: "One Englishman is a story. Ten Frenchmen is a story. One hundred Germans is a story. One thousand Indians is a story. Nothing ever happens in Chile."

American journalists may think of themselves as more progressive than their English cousins on Fleet Street. But the motto could as easily have been posted on the wall of a U.S. newsroom.

In 1962 the dean of the Ohio University journalism school noted that United Press International did not move a single dispatch from Chile during a month when that country experienced economic collapse and the Vatican selected a Chilean to be the youngest cardinal in history.

More than three decades later, a critic could easily chronicle similar problems with American media treatment of foreign news. Indeed, the two of us did so in a 1989 article, noting that television networks were cutting back on overseas coverage, that many large newspaper groups had no foreign correspondents, and that no full-time U.S. correspondents were "based in Bangladesh, Indonesia and Nigeria—three of the ten most populous countries in the world." Since then, the space devoted to foreign news has decreased, and news bureaus abroad reduced for financial reasons.

If newspapers are supposed to cover events relevant to Americans, foreign news should be high on their list of priorities. This is the age of global interdependence. American lives are tied to global competition, the global environment, and the amalgamation of rhythmic overseas music called "worldbeat."

Editors and readers, however, have good reasons for overlooking overseas news. One is history. Even with its involvement in world wars, the United States has been relatively insulated from the rest of the world for nearly two centuries. Another is money. Fielding a single foreign correspondent typically costs $250,000 or more a year. For that much money an editor could easily hire five or six local reporters and give them hefty expense accounts. And remember, one foreign correspondent can only do so much. To really report foreign news, a newspaper needs between twenty and thirty correspondents, who would still be spread very thinly over the world's nearly two hundred countries. Only the biggest newspapers, like the Los Angeles *Times,* can afford to dispatch large numbers of reporters overseas.

The approximately 1,550 U.S. newspapers that belong to the Associated Press and the many papers that subscribe to other news services run by large newspaper organizations have access to their foreign news reports. But those newspapers still have only limited space in which to run stories. No newspaper has sufficient room to publish even a short article about more than a handful of countries on a given day, and these give most attention to dramatic events such as revolutions, not to background issues. When newspapers increase foreign coverage, they usually do so with a regional slant. West Coast newspapers pay particular attention to countries on the Pacific Rim, with whom they have a booming trade. Newspapers in the Southwest and Florida favor Latin America. As a result of its immigrant population, Chicago papers carry a lot of news about the former Soviet bloc. Africa, meanwhile, gets short shrift in virtually all major daily newspapers. The common reasons given are, first, that U.S. trade with Africa is negligible and, second, that today's African Americans don't identify closely with the people and places.

The American public knows it is supposed to care about the rest of the world. But people are not always certain why. In opinion polls respondents *say* they are very interested in foreign news—at a much higher rate than editors predict. At the same time, study after study shows that Americans have so little understanding of foreign issues that they can't locate large countries on the map, let alone describe the central problems facing those countries.

The situation is perhaps best summed up by two comments on news from south of the border years ago. "The people of the United States will do anything for Latin America except read about it," said New York *Times* columnist James Reston. Responded the former U.S. ambassador to the Organization of American States, Sol Linowitz, "I don't believe that. I believe they will [read], but I think reporters will do anything for Latin America except write about it."

Whichever view one takes, intelligent readers know that they need more than their daily paper if they want to be informed about Chile.

## Why the Reporter Didn't Listen to Your Story

As noted in earlier sections of this book, the limitations of space may leave a relative's lengthy obituary on the cutting room floor. But that is not the only reason a near-and-dear story may not find its way into the paper.

The press jealously guards its prerogative to decide what goes into the paper. Your favorite story may seem like news to you. To an editor, it may just be special pleading, which is not news.

That proprietary attitude doesn't just stem from a sense of power and ego in the newsroom, although those are admittedly influential factors. It is more a matter of "news judgment"—a keystone of the journalistic craft.

Making decisions about what is newsworthy is a lot more complicated than it was just a couple of decades ago when a local reporter's territory barely extended beyond the police precinct, the courts, and city hall. Nowadays journalists turn up in such places as business boardrooms, rain forests, the halls of academia, and occasionally a politician's bedroom.

Thanks largely to technology, there is another factor complicating the news-decision process: a glut of information. Satellite transmission, telephone modems, and computerized databases have increased manifold the flood of data coming into today's newsroom. More than ever, editors perform the function of gatekeeper (and often feel like the boy with his finger in the dike).

Even if journalists weren't in the flood-control business, their priorities and values are often considerably different from members of the public trying to peddle their stories.

Let's take some typical examples:

1. A local conservation group wants to block a developer from filling in and building houses on a wetlands area that is a sanctuary for birds. The group appeals to the newspaper to publish an editorial opposing the development. The editorial director declines, saying more information is needed. The conservationists howl that the paper is "in the pocket of the developers."

2. A man who identifies himself as a freelance inventor appears in the newsroom and announces that he has found a safe alternative to nuclear power, but neither the energy industry nor the government gives him any attention. He is convinced there is a "conspiracy" to keep him quiet, and he asks that the newspaper expose it. A reporter interviews the inventor, makes two phone calls, and after consulting with the editor tells the inventor the paper is not going to pursue this story.

3. A photo of the high school marching band is published on the sports page. A parent writes a letter complaining to the editor that her

son's name was not mentioned in the photo caption, even though two others in the same row were mentioned. She wants to know why the paper is "discriminating" against her son.

What the reader is unlikely to know is that each of these alleged "shortcomings" may have arisen from a carefully thought-out decision by the newspaper (for better or for worse).

1. In the development case, the editorial director felt that the newspaper had not covered the issue thoroughly enough to justify taking an editorial position at this stage. There just wasn't enough reliable information. She also remembered hearing a comment recently about an "infestation of mosquitoes" in the area where the wetlands was located. So the reason for the turndown here was that the newspaper wasn't ready to publish the editorial.

2. In the inventor's case, the reporter—being skeptical by nature and somewhat jaundiced about conspiracy theories—listened patiently to the visitor. He asked specific questions about the invention and the people in industry and government whom the inventor had contacted. The inventor was a bit vague on names and dates and had very little documentation to back up his contention that no one would listen to him. The reporter took down as much information as possible and told the inventor he would be in touch after doing some research. After calling sources whom he trusted, the reporter became convinced that he was dealing with a "total nut case who wouldn't know a BTU from his butt," to use the words of one of his contacts at the Light and Power Authority. "He's been pestering us for years, and I can't tell you how much staff time he has taken up." So the reason for the turndown here was that the newspaper was unconvinced of the inventor's claims.

3. The photo identification problem was primarily a matter of priorities. The photo editor had identified the two most central figures in the picture, one of them being the band leader and the other the drum major. He left three others unidentified because he couldn't fit all the names into the allocated caption space.* "It was a judgment call," the editor explained. "Next time, I'll think twice about identifying any of them!" So the reason for the turndown was that the newspaper has space limitations, prompting choices all the time as to what goes in and what goes out.

---

* It's also possible the photographer didn't take down all the names at the time.

The three stories mentioned above are all fictional, but similar ones happen daily in newsrooms across the country. They help explain why journalists have a heightened sense of cynicism about the public. Reporters regularly deal with pushy and devious types trying to manipulate, spin, and sell the news. They also attract a disproportionate share of kooks in search of fame and fortune. Of course, some might say this is poetic justice for a business that expends so much of its own energy seeking out the bizarre, the loud, and the deviant.

## Why a Falling Tree Doesn't Make News Unless a Reporter Hears It

Everyone knows the old philosophical conundrum: "Does a falling tree make noise if no one hears it?" However you may answer *that* question, the answer to its journalistic analogue is not in doubt. There are newsworthy events everywhere, around the world and in our own backyards. But where there are no journalists, or on-the-spot observers who supply journalists with details, there is no news.

This need "to be there" is why journalists favor sunshine laws that give them access to government meetings. It is why they cultivate sources for what is happening behind the scenes. It is also why people who want to shape the news spend a lot of time chopping down trees in such a way that journalists can't avoid them.

Although the public often feels it has little control over the news, citizens can manipulate journalistic routines and rituals to their own advantage. Here are some of the ways sources orchestrate news.

The first, most basic step is *advancing* stories. Journalists, like everyone else, want to know what is going to happen before it actually occurs. Among other things, it is easier for journalists to do a story when they can plan for it. Thus editors keep what are sometimes called "daybooks" in which they list upcoming events. The city editor, for instance, will refer to the daybook when giving daily instructions to general assignment reporters. Reporters with their own beats keep their own calendars of upcoming stories. Sources go to pains to help by sending advance announcements to editors and reporters or even by calling to remind them what is coming.

*Press releases* take advancing one step further. They alert journalists to a story and, at the same time, give the source of the release a chance to highlight those aspects of the story it considers most important. A typical press release will be full of quotes and statistics that journalists can use. Reporters are supposed to go beyond the release and develop their own stories; some of the less professional newspapers will run a routine press release verbatim.

Timing counts for a lot in orchestrating the news. Lord Dawson of Penn, physician to King George V, understood this very well indeed, as he made clear in diary notes that came to light many years later. When the king was close to death in 1936, Dawson administered a lethal combination of morphine and cocaine. The resulting timely death ensured that the news would appear first in the *Times*, "rather than the less appropriate evening journals." To make certain nothing would go amiss, Dawson had his wife alert the royal *Times* that the announcement was coming.

While euthanasia is a bit extreme, sources do routinely pay attention to the timing of press releases. Sometimes they do this to hold back information for a while; often they do so to guarantee that a large number of journalists report the story.* The standard technique is to place an *embargo* on the release. An embargo prohibits editors from running the story until a certain date (and, usually, time). This ensures wide distribution of the release while minimizing the chance that one newspaper will run the story before everyone else and thus detract from its news value for those who hold off. Journalists honor the embargo for several reasons. The embargo gives them time to develop a cogent story. Also, violation of the embargo would bring opprobrium from other journalists and could result in being frozen out by the source in the future.** Embargoes also can be placed on

---

* Note, however, that it is sometimes wise to give an advance story as an exclusive to a reporter. The reporter, having it all to him- or herself, is more inclined to play it up. George Washington gave an advance copy of his famous Farewell Address to a friendly newspaper, *Claypoole's American Daily Advertiser.*

** Only on rare occasions will reporters break ranks with colleagues. Should someone unaware of the embargo run the story, a reporter generally feels free to write the story immediately. One of the most celebrated cases of breaking ranks occurred at the end of World War II. A handful of journalists were allowed to visit the signing of the German surrender at Reims, but were told they could not report the event until given permission from the general in charge of public relations. The AP's Edward Kennedy wrote the story anyway. The New York *Times* carried the story on its front page on Tuesday. On Thursday it ran an editorial accusing Kennedy of a "grave disservice to the newspaper profession."

speeches, documents such as the federal government's annual budget, and even on publication of books like this one.

Embargoes play to journalists' preference for breaking news. A set release time gives the appearance of an event: "The Association for Tire Manufacturers *today* reported that . . ." But an even better way to give reporters a falling tree to cover is a *news conference.*

News conferences pose some risks for those who call them. Journalists can ask questions, often uncomfortable ones. But the event gives organizers a chance to get their message across in their own way, and this lets them shape news. The people who call news conferences don't bring their critics to the podium.

News conferences work only if journalists come. For most high-profile leaders this is not a problem. Public officials, heads of large associations, and business leaders can expect a good turnout if they have a reputation of offering information substantially interesting to reporters. But for some smaller, less well known groups or individuals, a press conference will not attract reporters. Homeless people, antiwar activists, and others with special causes protest in front of the White House every day—some even live there in makeshift tents—and the press walks by them each morning en route to the White House briefing room.

This does not mean that antiestablishment groups can never make news. There are other ways to stage events besides news conferences. *Demonstrations, sit-ins,* and *marches* are designed to get news attention for a point of view; often they are more newsworthy than a news conference. AIDS victims, for instance, may feel their plight does not get sufficient government support. They may not at the moment have a study to release that would warrant a press conference. But a large march in Washington, with placards protesting government neglect, is likely to attract media attention, which in turn may develop public concern and generate more government action.

Terrorists have learned the same lesson. They bomb buildings not because they are primarily interested in maiming people and destroying property. Their main objective is to make news, to draw attention to their concerns, and to shape the policies of their adversaries. In this they can be hugely successful. In the early 1970s the tiny Symbionese Liberation Army (SLA) kidnapped Patricia Hearst, daughter of the publisher of the San Francisco *Examiner.* A media critic at the time noted that the *Examiner* "has bent over backward to publish without comment every 'communiqué' from the SLA."

Most reporters are cheerful about embargoes and press conferences by the Establishment. These devices are part of the news routine. But when terrorists try to manipulate the news, journalists grow uneasy.

••••••••••••••••••••••••••••••••••••••••••••••••••••••••••••••••

### Aside: Five Ways to Make News

With government agencies, legislators, and special interest groups vying for attention, it's often necessary to be creative. Here are five ways to wheedle your way into the newspaper.

*Tie the story to one that reporters have to cover.* If you want to issue a report on joblessness, wait until the first Friday of the month. That is the day the Labor Department issues its monthly unemployment statistics, and journalists are always looking for a fresh angle when reporting that routine story. Your report will be worth at least a few sentences, starting something like: "In a related development today . . ."

*Concoct a photo opportunity.* When the public relations staff at the Agency for International Development wanted to draw attention to the money they saved during the year, they arranged what around the White House is called a photo opportunity. Pictures of the president receiving a government agency report rarely make it into the paper. But this one was different. The head of AID presented the president with a five-foot-long mock-up of a check that showed the millions being returned to John and Jane Q. Public. Photo editors are always prowling around for a sparkling picture to dress up the paper; even cynical editors use this kind of picture.

*Give reporters and editors an angle they can't resist.* If you want to make an announcement on legislation to curb noise pollution, hold a press conference near a construction site where jackhammers are rattling away. New York senator Charles Goodell did that years ago, and reporters and their editors couldn't resist leads like this: "Nearly drowned out by noise, Senator Goodell announced today . . ."

*Plant the idea as a rumor.* Journalists love to hunt down the truth in rumor. One New England congressman took advantage of this years ago. When news broke that a cabinet officer had resigned, he had his press secretary call a reporter. "Listen," the aide said, "we've been getting calls all morning from reporters saying that my boss is in line for the job. Confidentially, we haven't heard anything directly from the White House yet, but could you do me a favor and check it out?"

The reporter called his paper's correspondent at the White House, who in turn asked his colleagues. By 4 P.M. the legislator's name was buzzing around the White House press corps. The president's press secretary said he couldn't comment on the matter until the president was ready to make his announcement, which fueled speculation even more. By 7 P.M. the legislator's name was one of three mentioned on the network evening news as being in the running, and the White House staff was considering him. Although the legislator wasn't the final choice, he had no complaint. He had plenty of publicity to impress folks back home.

*Become president.* When the news media found out George Bush didn't like broccoli, they jumped on the story. Virtually everything you do as president is news.

• • • • • • • • • • • • • • • • • • • • • • • • • • • • • • • • • • • • • • • • • • • • • • •

## Why Journalists Like People More Than Ideas

Every time there's a presidential campaign, politicians complain the media pay too much attention to personalities and not enough to issues. Voters voice the same complaints in letters to the editor and calls to talk shows.

Journalists tend to agree. They spend a lot of time scolding themselves when the election returns are in and they have time for reflection. Then they go right out and do the same thing all over again.

Journalists know ideas are important. Many are experimenting in campaign coverage to reshape what one news guru calls the "hunter-gatherer" newsroom culture that accentuates the collection of information and downplays its significance. But even those most interested in changing course must fight powerful crosswinds that push journalists in the direction of personality reporting not only in politics but generally.

One reason is readability. Ideas *are* often boring or at least dry. "Reporters often complain that they cannot write about an important government program—general revenue sharing, for instance—because there are no people in it," commented Calvin Trillin. The common refrain in the newsroom is to "get the human interest angle," to make the abstract seem real.

This search for human interest angles is seductive. Consider this May, 1993, Associated Press report:

> Eight months after losing his mother to alcohol poisoning, an 8-year-old boy watched helplessly as lightning struck his father and killed him during a visit to her grave.
>
> Bobby J. Lowe, 39, of Arbutus, and his son, Joey, had just finished placing a flower on the grave of Laura Fauver when a band of violent thunderstorms moved into the area Wednesday night, police said.
>
> With lightning and thunder rumbling through the area, the father and son sought shelter under a large pine tree at the Loudon Park Cemetery in southwest Baltimore.
>
> Soon after, a lightning bolt hit the tree, splitting it down the middle and then striking Lowe, apparently hitting him on the St. Christopher's medal that was hanging from his neck, officer Craig Rossmark said.

It is not big news when a child loses a second parent, tragic as that is. But when the facts create a little human drama, as this one did, complete with the irony of the St. Christopher medal attracting lightning, the story becomes irresistible—and runs in newspapers across the country.

Many echo the sentiment of the British protagonist of the novel *Ruggles of Red Gap:* "Again I was brought to marvel at a peculiarity of the American press, a certain childish eagerness for marvels and grotesque wonders." They also complain that in focusing on people, the press trivializes important news. When a Supreme Court nominee is rejected for having tried marijuana as a college student, critics blame the press for having derailed serious review of the nominee's qualifications. When an article about a visiting prime minister devotes a full paragraph to what she was wearing, letters pour in from irate readers complaining the newspaper would not give a man that treatment—and besides, who cares?

Many blame television for accentuating this kind of reporting. When he was chairman of the Federal Communications Commission, Alfred C. Sikes pointed out how even the best TV news program skirts serious issues. Drawing attention to one of the best, *Nightline* on ABC, he noted that in the 1980s Ted Koppel devoted only 6 shows out of 1,850 to the federal deficit and 8 shows to strange animals, 8 to fatness and hair loss, and 9 to Elvis, rock 'n' roll, and video.

But people like stories about people. Witness the success of *People* magazine and the comparatively low readership of the issue-oriented *New Republic*. Even serious-minded readers want information about people. A trivial story to one reader is highly meaningful to another. Many sophisticated readers, for example, think the personal lives of political leaders have a bearing on their ability to govern. True, a politician's sex life bears no relevance to the merits of his or her platform, but many think it says something profound about character. Even a political leader's off-color joke can become news. In 1974, Secretary of Agriculture Earl Butz told this one, which was widely reported: An Italian woman is asked about the pope's stand on birth control and replies, "He no play-a the game, he no make-a the rules." Many readers thought Butz's joke was offensive and suggested he was unfit for high public office. Later, when he made an obscene racial joke, he lost his job.

The *Wall Street Journal* and *Christian Science Monitor* are among the prestigious publications that examine how major issues affect daily lives. In their own ways, both have perfected a technique called "case history" reporting, which spotlights a single individual as a metaphor for a social trend, economic policy, or political development.

"If we define journalism as the chronicle of human thoughts and actions, it has to be about people," says former *Monitor* correspondent Kristin Helmore. She notes the special importance of this kind of journalism for self-governing societies: "When stories are told and word-pictures painted of a [particular] project's impact on individual lives, readers respond, and may even be stirred to action."

## Why You Read So Much About Homeless Cats

Like the people who run them, newspapers have personalities with quirks, foibles, and preferences. Sometimes the management is eccentric; sometimes it is the newspaper's philosophy that produces peculiarities. Sometimes readers won't see an idiosyncrasy at work on a story, but often they can develop a feel for what motivates a newspaper.

Newspapers' personalities are easiest to spot. The New York *Post* is intentionally sensational, full of stories about crime and the bizarre.

The editors see their working-class audience wanting entertainment and a voice for its frustrations. The *Christian Science Monitor* was created as an antidote to "yellow journalism." It strives for a serious, humane tone appealing to a liberal, educated readership. Other papers are a reflection of the owner's political persuasion, such as the outspokenly conservative Manchester *Union Leader* in New Hampshire, founded by the late William Loeb, the man who made Ed Muskie cry.*

A newspaper's little indulgences are sometimes less obvious. Let's say the paper has a lot of stories about homeless cats. Why? Perhaps the publisher or his wife have a thing about abandoned animals. Or say the paper gives a lot of attention to community fire protection. Could it be the editor is a volunteer fireman?

For many years the New York *Times* gave special attention to one subject, beautification. Iphigene Ochs Sulzburger, the matriarch of the owning family, was devoted to sprucing up public places. Consequently, the *Times* newsroom did not take this subject lightly. Harrison Salisbury, one of the paper's star foreign correspondents, came back from a posting in Russia with a Pulitzer Prize. One of his first assignments was to cover sanitation.

For the Hederman family, which owned morning and evening dailies in Jackson, Mississippi, the issue was booze. As staunch Baptists, the Hedermans took a dim view of liquor. No reporter dared turn in an expense form that included charges for a martini at lunch. At considerable expense to themselves, the Hedermans' *Clarion-Ledger* and the *Daily News* refused to take any liquor advertisements. They also used their influence to press for state laws that forbade other publications printed in Mississippi to print liquor ads.

The Block family's Toledo newspaper, the *Blade,* lobbies hard for the state to situate more government offices in the city. The paper's editorials complain that Ohio's government ignores Toledo, and the publisher has testified to the same effect before the state legislature. But the family's enthusiasm doesn't stop there. As reporters privately admit, they feel pressure to introduce the topic whenever possible in the news pages and put a positive spin on it.

---

\* Democratic presidential candidate Edmund Muskie showed tears of anger and frustration during a 1972 press conference in New Hampshire in which he complained about Loeb's criticism of Muskie's wife. Muskie's poor showing in the New Hampshire primary is widely attributed to the "crying" incident.

The Chicago *Tribune*'s Colonel Robert "Bertie" McCormick was as colorful as they come. He had a penchant for military trappings (he served under General John J. Pershing in World War I) and riding outfits (which he sometimes wore to work). Although he had a British tailor, hatter, and shoemaker, wore a British-style moustache, and spoke with a slight British accent, he was outspokenly anti-British, a sentiment that showed up in *Tribune* news coverage. Traditional English spelling, he thought, needed American reform, and he used his newspaper to launch a crusade. *Freight, though, phantom, island,* and *catalogue,* among many other words, became *frate, tho, fantom, iland,* and *catalog.* The *Tribune* went back to standard spellings in 1974. But this was nearly 20 years after the colonel passed away, and some of his eccentric spellings, like *catalog,* had by then become widely accepted.

Author and journalist Joseph Mitchell tells the story of his old employer, the late New York *Herald Tribune,* whose owners forbade use of the word *blood* in stories. This made it difficult to cover gangland killings such as one where a "little establishment looked as if blood had been shot in through a hose."

Even the *Christian Science Monitor,* which prides itself on responsible reporting, has a strong bias against medical affairs. This policy is set by the Christian Science church, its owner, which discourages the use of doctors and medicine. The paper did adjust to the AIDS epidemic, however. After a lot of soul-searching in the newsroom, the *Monitor* began devoting attention to this public health menace.

Rarely does a paper explain why it gave a story front-page play or extensive coverage, even if the decision has created stormy controversy in the newsroom. In that sense, journalism is much like theater. The audience isn't supposed to see what's happening backstage. Readers generally were not aware of the wrenching agony inside the Washington *Post* over its Watergate coverage and inside the New York *Times* in 1971 before it published the Pentagon Papers, classified government documents outlining United States involvement in Vietnam.

But newspapers' personalities do shape the news. Some predilections get in the way; some make the newspaper more interesting and produce good reporting. Salisbury tackled his city trash assignment for the New York *Times* with gusto. His series on New York garbage collection won him another award.

# Why Papers Prefer Their Own Stories

Newspapers prefer to publish stories written by their own staff journalists rather than those written by somebody else's reporter. What's the point of paying reporters if you don't use them? Editors also believe their own staff can do the best job, and they know the strengths and weaknesses of their own reporters better than they know reporters for other organizations. Besides, if our press is as independent as it claims to be, it's natural for a newspaper to want its own unique product.

There's a lot of truth to these arguments. But they leave out the intensely human quality of pride.

True enough, newspapers can't have their own reporters everywhere there is news. The smaller the newspaper, the more dependent it is on help from wire services and syndicates, the country's information wholesalers. But when a really big story comes along, dispatching one's own staff writer to cover the event gives a newspaper a sense of pride. That is why thousands of journalists are accredited to the annual Super Bowl, to the political conventions every four years, and to the occasional foreign war, at extraordinary cost to newspaper owners. Editors justify these splurges by saying they need the "local angle"—coverage of the hometown fans, delegation, troops, etc. But the primary motive usually has less to do with serving the reader than with promoting the newspaper—getting that hometown byline (the writer's name) above the big story with the tag "Gazette Staff Correspondent." That's seen as the kind of major league stuff that wins prizes.

For editors at the prestige papers, few things hurt as much as having to print the phrase "From News Services" or "Wire Dispatches." The preferred rule is, if the story is worth the front page, our people should be writing it. When they don't get the story themselves, they are more inclined to bury the wire version inside the paper or just ignore it. Smaller papers are more willing to run wire service stories even on local events. Newspapers commonly rewrite the first few paragraphs of a wire service report, maybe adding a fact or two, and publish the story as their own.*

---

\* Newspaper reporters say this is fair play. The AP seldom credits "pick-ups" from newspapers, a practice permitted in its cooperative agreement with member papers. The broadcast media don't credit any outsiders unless they have to— such as a copyrighted exclusive by another network or newspaper.

Of course, it's perilous to generalize. Some large metropolitan newspapers are less proprietary about their reporting. The Chicago *Tribune,* for one, makes fairly liberal use of wire copy. This frees up its own correspondents to ferret out other news or delve deeper into the top story.

The examples are endless of a proprietary mentality distorting the news. One arose when President Clinton was selecting an attorney general. The Washington *Post* was slow to respond to the growing controversy over nominee Zoe Baird's possible violation of labor laws governing immigrant workers. The New York *Times* "broke" the first story, and the *Post*'s executive editor conceded his paper "may have been less than enthusiastic about chasing a rival's exclusive."

Do readers really care which paper got the story first or whose name appears over it? Most surveys say no. Readers are loyal to their favorite columnists and feature writers, but generally they don't care who writes most of the stuff. It is the reporters who watch bylines and editors who care most about having their own people on the scene. After all, they don't want the head of some other paper to have more to brag about at the annual editors' convention.

## Why a Family Newspaper Doesn't Say "Shit"

Anyone looking for a solid, God-fearing family man in the community of journalists need go no further than Charles Alexander. We know this. We are good friends with Charlie, an elder in the Presbyterian church, since the time he felt forced to leave the Dayton *Journal Herald* for publishing foul language. To us, he is also a vivid example of the limits often placed on a family paper.

The story of Charlie's abrupt departure from the Dayton *Journal Herald* centered on the killing of one local Treasury Department agent by another, Casper Carroll Gibson. The paper obtained a copy of Gibson's affidavit. Excerpts, which ran in the newspaper, included this, in which Gibson said: "His lips were drawn back cross his teeth, and he was screaming at me. And he screamed something to the effect, 'Gibson, God damn it, you are fucking with my family. You are fucking with my future. I am not going to let you do it. I'll kill you first.'" According to Gibson, his colleague then pulled a gun from his pocket. Gibson "grabbed with both hands and pushed it, and there was a terrible roar, the damn gun went off."

Charlie defended the decision to use the word *fucking* on the grounds that it conveyed the essence of the event being reported, a man "blind with rage." The Cox family, who owned the Dayton *Journal Herald,* did not agree. The word, they said, was "indefensible." Charlie resigned.

The dictionary definition of *dilemma* is "a choice between equally bad alternatives." In matters of taste and morals, editors often face dilemmas.

The average daily newspaper sees itself as a family newspaper. Not only does it go to people with different points of view, but it's meant to be read by all members of the family. With their claims of serving the public, these newspapers have an obligation not to encourage antisocial behavior. They also have a financial interest in not offending the religious or moral convictions of readers, who can cancel their subscriptions.

On the other hand, the real world of news is often offensive. And what offends one person may be interesting to another customer.

Editors have long known that a little cheesecake, to use a common phrase, sells newspapers. That's why *Sports Illustrated* runs a swimsuit issue each year. Editors also know, however, that many people (ranging from feminists to those who prefer traditional roles for women) object to showing buxom women ready to plunge into the surf. Al Neuharth saw the benefit of mixing wholesome with buxom in *USA Today.* He is once supposed to have been disappointed that the photo of a comely woman ran at the bottom of the front page. "The next time you run a picture of a nice, clean-cut All-American girl in a tight sweater," he commanded, "get her tits above the fold."

Or consider how squeamish editors can be over words much less offensive than the f-word. In what became a major news story in 1993, a Virginia woman cut off her husband's penis with a 12-inch kitchen knife in retaliation for what she claimed was sexual abuse. Some newspapers used the word *penis* in headlines. Others looked hard for euphemisms: *mutilation,* for instance, and *offending organ.* About the same time the Los Angeles *Times* came out with its 19-page "Guidelines on Ethnic, Racial, Sexual and Other Identification." Eager not to offend anyone, it banned such words and phrases as *Chinese fire drill, crazy, dark continent, Eskimo,* and *welsher. Birth defect,* the guide said, should be replaced with *congenital disability.*

Here are some particularly difficult decisions editors have faced when deciding what should go into their family newspapers.

• During the war in Vietnam an Associated Press photographer, Nick Ut, was on hand when the South Vietnamese military accidentally napalmed its own civilians. One of his pictures showed a panic-stricken naked girl running away from the flames. In retrospect most would agree on the news merits of the picture. It won a Pulitzer Prize and became one of the most searing images of the war. But at the time of its publication reporters and editors alike wondered about using the shot, which showed full, frontal nudity.

• Another war-related episode occurred more recently. When the United States became involved in Somalia, the initial motive was humanitarian relief. U.S. troops were brought in to ensure that civil war conflict did not prevent food from reaching the starving. Eventually, though, military personnel became involved in the fighting itself, and one captured American pilot was dragged through the streets of Mogadishu. Journalists caught that event on film. Some editors ran the photo; some buried it inside the newspaper; some refused to use the photo at all, believing it needlessly disturbed readers.

• Editors agonize over news that may lead people to hurt themselves. Not long ago Walt Disney released a film called *The Program.* In it football players lie in the middle of a busy thoroughfare to prove they have guts. When real-life teenagers repeated the prank, serious injury and death followed. Walt Disney decided to cut the scene from the movie, but news media problems had only begun. Television news clips showed the scene, and newspapers wrote about both the film and what TV news was doing. This resulted in publicizing a movie that had poor reviews and was attracting few viewers but that had prompted newsworthy events.

• In 1994 a photographer snapped a poignant picture at the anniversary of the Woodstock festival. In it a woman is looking distastefully at a nude man sitting in a lawn chair. The photographer's newspaper, the Washington *Times,* did not use the picture. This is "a family newspaper," said the managing editor. Subsequently, however, the photo won first prize in the White House News Photographers Association competition.

• Until the 1950s most newspapers wouldn't even use the word *rape,* and even though that taboo is now broken, many reporters and editors have remained puritanical on sexual matters. Not so long ago the Bluefield *Daily Telegraph* in West Virginia did not include the nationally distributed *USA Weekend* magazine with its Sunday paper. In the cover photo, three kindergarten children were holding vegetables to illustrate an article on good nutrition; an editor thought that a carrot looked too phallic. "The cover depicts an image that violates this newspaper's family standards," said the editor later.

• A generation ago newspapers rarely discussed homosexuality. Today many are not certain what to do. Gays have become a more visible part of our society. Many readers, however, say covering gay issues violates family values and is tantamount to condoning "deviant behavior." When the Detroit *News* announced it would run the nation's first column devoted to gay issues, 353 readers canceled their subscriptions. Within the next month 157 more dropped their subscriptions. "We're not trying to titillate but educate and explain what often are very difficult changes in society," editor Bob Giles said. "Gay families are just an extension of the family concept."

Perhaps nothing has opened newspapers to sex-related topics as much as the Acquired Immune Deficiency Syndrome (AIDS). More and more it seems irresponsible *not* to be explicit about sex. The public, including young people, are at risk from AIDS. And feeling at risk, the public is ripe for all sorts of misunderstandings and even panic: "Should I stop eating at restaurants where someone with AIDS might be serving food?" Meanwhile, health officials have created public information campaigns to counsel people on the need to use condoms and to discourage certain kinds of sexual activity. Most editors have felt obliged to discuss sexually transmitted disease in some detail.

Newspapers typically have their own policies on use of profanity and other "family" issues. Most would say that your family newspaper doesn't say "shit" unless it is absolutely essential to the story. Even then editors may not find owners in agreement. But, as Charlie learned, there is life after such disagreements. He became a professor at Northwestern University's Medill School of Journalism, where he has distinguished himself by molding responsible new journalists.

# V

......................................

# News Sources

# Why Journalists Don't Quote Themselves

A fire breaks out in the Associated Press headquarters in New York City. The AP reports the blaze to the fire department. But when it comes time to report the story for readers, AP reporters act as though they never saw the fire. They interview a fire department spokesman for details about the blaze.

When a night cashier is found stabbed to death in the Washington *Post* cafeteria, none of the newspaper's reporters are quoted in the story published the next day. The *Post* reporters assigned to the story interview the police, who give the facts of the murder.

From their first day on the job, journalists are told to report facts and keep both themselves and their opinions out of the news. The idea is ingrained in them by editors the way drill sergeants drum into recruits that they must march in step. To establish they are not just making up information, reporters find authorities or written reports and documents to which they can attribute facts. Attribution, as it is called, is the reporter's security blanket.

The beauty of attribution is that it allows the reporter to introduce opinions into a story without losing the appearance of neutrality. A reporter will not say that President Bush is lying about his lack of involvement in the Reagan administration's arms-for-hostages deal with Iran, an issue that dogged Bush throughout his term. But the reporter can quote someone else who says that the president is lying. The reporter is reporting a fact, to wit the fact that someone holds a certain opinion. Should it subsequently become incontrovertibly clear that George Bush has told the truth, the reporter is safe. The reporter stuck to the facts. The fault lies with the source.

As with other aspects of journalism, good reporters understand they cannot introduce an opinion into the story just because they can attribute it to someone else. It makes a difference who that person is. If the attribution is simply from the man or woman on the street, who has no inside information about President Bush, the opinion means nothing. If the reporter uses someone who worked closely with Bush when he was vice president, it means a great deal. That's why it was front-page news in the fall of 1992 when a former National Security Council aide said that he had told Bush previously that the United States was trading arms with Iran.

Most news organizations have at least a two-source rule for information that is likely to be highly sensational. If different sources won't corroborate the story, the newspaper won't go with it. This can result in stories being withheld for a few days, even forever.

As an example, consider the Washington *Post*'s 1992 investigation of charges that Senator Bob Packwood sexually harassed women staffers. The story could have made the difference in the senator's successful reelection bid, but the paper did not print the story until several weeks after the ballots were cast. The *Post* ombudsman, Joann Byrd, explained why: "An investigation project of this sensitivity cannot be turned around for tomorrow's newspaper. Finding the people who had relevant experiences is itself complicated. . . . And for this story, the incidents the women described were not witnessed by third parties. In the routines of reporting, each recollection then needs independent corroboration, typically by several others who must themselves be located and persuaded to talk."

The news reporter's need to locate sources, gain their trust, and persuade them to talk creates a complicated web of relationships that the following sections explore.

## Why the Ship of State Leaks

The juiciest facts, virtually by definition, are typically those few people know and, if they know them, are typically unwilling to say much about for fear they will get into trouble. To acquire those facts, journalists will strike a bargain with sources: in exchange for the precious information, they will hold back other information, the identity of the source.

One of the most celebrated cases of a source's reluctance to be identified occurred during the Watergate investigation of President Richard Nixon. Bob Woodward, a young Washington *Post* reporter, cultivated a source with ties well inside the White House. So careful was Woodward to protect his source, called "Deep Throat," that he did not reveal the name to his editors or even to his reporting partner, Carl Bernstein. Nor has he since publicly identified Deep Throat. "Any reporter who's ever had a good source knows how important and vital sources are to the news business," Woodward said on the twentieth anniversary of the Watergate break-in. "My feelings about this [need to protect sources] are almost ecclesiastical."

Deep Throat helped Woodward win a Pulitzer Prize and President Nixon lose his job. And Nixon is not the only president to rue the use of anonymous sources. All recent presidents have complained about aides anonymously giving inside information to the press. As President Kennedy once wryly commented, the "ship of state is the only ship that leaks from the top."

Don't feel too sorry, however, for presidents or other officials who get blasted by anonymous sources. Most political leaders and officials really don't dislike leaks as much as they say they do. They dislike leaks they haven't controlled.

As for journalists, even those who dislike the terms of confidentiality find it difficult not to play along with "informed sources." They need information, and this is a good way to get it. Studies have found that as many as one-third of the stories in a typical newspaper use anonymous quotes.

Journalists' use of anonymous sources has all the ritual of a Japanese tea ceremony. Naturally a lingo goes with it. Here are some of the key phrases:

• *Off the record,* which means the information is only for the reporter's edification and not for publication. Some say the reporter can use the material "to pry information out of other people involved in the story." Some say a reporter cannot use off-the-record information even "as leverage to obtain it from another source." In many cases such information is offered as a way to explain a particular set of circumstances that should not be publicized at the moment or to give the journalist forewarning of a story about to break.

• *Background,* which means the same thing as *not for attribution.* The reporter can use the information but can't use the source's name. Diplomats, for instance, are well known for speaking to reporters on condition they won't be quoted by name later. If they step on diplomatic toes, they can avoid blame. The envoys also can float controversial ideas. If a trial balloon falls like a lead weight thanks to negative public opinion, the source is still safe. And, of course, the reporter still has a story.

When using this technique, reporters attribute the information very broadly to "well-informed sources" or "senior officials." When officials are particularly wary of being identified, they speak on *deep background*, a term coined by Secretary of State Dean Rusk. Under these rules, reporters cannot use any attribution whatsoever. That is similar to Bob Woodward's arrangement with Deep Throat, who agreed to "confirm information that had been obtained elsewhere." Woodward, in turn, agreed not even to indicate in his news stories at the time that he relied on Deep Throat as an anonymous source.

• *On the record*, which reporters prefer. Whatever the source says is fair game and can be fully attributed.

The use of anonymous sources helps get sensitive facts into the public eye. It offers a safe way for whistleblowers to alert journalists to some corporate or government wrongdoing.

Yet anonymous sources can also be used to the opposite effect—to avoid the hard work of reporting. A reporter who can't substantiate a fact can claim an anonymous source. A notorious example occurred at the Washington *Post* in the early 1980s. Janet Cooke, a reporter on the paper (who worked for Bob Woodward), wrote a powerful story about an eight-year-old heroin addict she identified as "Jimmy." Cooke told her editors she could not give the boy's full name because she had promised him and his mother anonymity. She also told the editors that the mother's boyfriend threatened her life if anyone identified the real Jimmy. The problem was that Cooke had made up Jimmy and his family. Cooke, whose story had won a Pulitzer Prize, was fired. The *Post* lost the Pulitzer Prize.

Leaks are tantalizing to reporters, who often get the information exclusively. "High officials," often adept at courting reporters, use anonymity to advance their private agendas. In the worst cases anonymous sources plant false information without taking any responsibility for their remarks. Officials try to win battles within an administration by selective leaks that derail or redirect policies.

Leaking techniques can have all the crafty subterfuge of a CIA counterintelligence operation. White House reporter Maureen Dowd relates this tactic:

> One Reagan official, whenever he wanted to leak a story, would throw in Don Regan's trademark phrase, "and the like," several times to insure that any quotes from an unidentified White House official would sound like the chief of staff. Similarly someone wanting [budget czar] Dick Darman to get the blame would toss in a word like "inchoate." If you read an unflattering anecdote about President Clinton that features the phrase "meaningful exchange" in an anonymous quote, don't assume Al Gore is the leaker; look for his enemy.

Journalists have developed techniques to keep anonymity to a minimum. The Associated Press has possibly the toughest rules. It will use an anonymous statement of fact provided that it is not available from any other source and that the story makes clear the source would not provide the information on the record. AP also will not permit the use of anonymous expressions of opinion.

Some have tried to go further. The editor of the Cincinnati *Enquirer* once noted he would not allow anonymous sources on the front page of the paper without his permission or the permission of his managing editor. At one point Ben Bradlee, editor of the Washington *Post,* decried the practice of background briefings as "vehicles for the government to give the press its version of the news." He told reporters "to make every reasonable effort to attribute information to its source."

But the problem is not so easily addressed as these rules might suggest. AP staffers have worried that restrictions on the use of anonymous sources actually result in a pro-government bias. The *Enquirer* rule on front-page anonymous sources is arbitrary and, as the editor admitted, "has pushed some pretty good stories back into the newspaper." And as much as Bradlee and other editors may say they want to boycott background briefings, anonymity is virtually impossible to resist—by either the press or the government. The arrangement is simply too convenient for each side, as an episode in 1992 highlighted.

During a news conference one day George Bush lamented widespread leaks from inside the White House: "What I'd say to the

American people is: Please ask for a name to be placed next to the source so I can get mad at the guy who's doing this." The next day presidential press secretary Marlin Fitzwater announced that Assistant Secretary of State Edward Djerejian would brief reporters on a meeting between Bush and King Hussein of Jordan under the following rules: Djerejian could only be quoted as "a senior administration official." When the White House press pointed out the contradiction with Bush's pronouncement the day before, the meeting was canceled. Administration officials released a four-paragraph statement and answered further questions on background only. Whatever irritation journalists may have felt at the administration talking out both sides of its mouth, they didn't troop out of the White House.

••••••••••••••••••••••••••••••••••••••••••••••••••••••••••••••••••••••••••••

### Aside: Why Reporters Won't Talk

In 1976 the New York *Times*'s Myron A. Farber reported on mysterious deaths at a New Jersey hospital. His articles led to the indictment of a physician on charges of poisoning five patients. When the defense subpoenaed Farber's notes, the judge asked to review the materials himself. The reporter and his paper refused. Both were fined. Farber spent forty days in jail for contempt.

This is not an isolated case. A Memphis *Commercial-Appeal* reporter wouldn't reveal the sources for a story on child abuse. A state senate committee cited him for contempt. A reporter for the *Tribune Chronicle* in Warren, Ohio, refused to testify before a grand jury about her interview with an indicted county engineer. She was jailed for twenty-two days.

The journalistic creed on protecting anonymous sources runs deep, so deep that journalists often will not reveal the names of criminals even if it means going to jail themselves. Betray your sources, journalists argue, and no one will talk to you again off the record. As a New York *Times* editorial said about the Farber case, "We contend that the First Amendment's protection of the press extends to the gathering as well as the printing of news. Frightened, threatened, or embarrassed sources daily offer our reporters fact, confession, rumor or accusation on condition that their identity remain secret. To betray one such source would jeopardize all."

Shield laws in roughly half the states in the country affirm this creed, although with various twists of their own. Many don't protect reporters in Farber's situation on the grounds that defendants are entitled to all the information bearing on their case.

In contrast, <u>courts have recently indicated that journalists are obligated to protect sources to whom they have promised anonymity</u>. Reporters with the Minneapolis *Star Tribune* and the St. Paul *Pioneer Press and Dispatch* promised a political figure confidentially for information on campaign dirty tricks. The editors decided their readers should know his identity because he was linked to the opposing candidate. The source, who lost his job, sued over the broken promise and, after the case was heard by the U.S. Supreme Court, won $200,000 in compensatory damages.

............................................................................

# Why the Press and Politicians Quarrel But Don't Divorce

If you are not in the Washington *Post* every day, you might as well not exist.

—Newt Gingrich

In 1890, on the last day of February, a former congressman visiting the Capitol encountered a newsman whose stories he did not like. The legislator pulled the reporter's nose. The journalist took out a gun and shot the legislator dead.

Here, it might seem, is the perfect metaphor for the relationship between journalists and politicians. When the press and those they cover face off, their antagonism can turn nasty. One of the leaders of the Washington press corps in the 1970s, Peter Lisagor of the Chicago *Daily News,* used to say half-jokingly to his colleagues, "Okay, boys, let's cut 'em up."

But another scene reveals just as much. The press conference is over, the television klieg lights doused. The journalist and the politician banter lightheartedly, ask about each other's kids, and maybe even go out to have a drink. Their quarrels are like lovers' spats, intense but not about to lead to divorce.

Inevitably, journalists write stories politicians don't like. Some can be demeaning and highly personal. Every time Gerald Ford stumbled, he landed in the newspaper.* President Nixon so hated the press that hounded him that he once said to confidants, "One day we will get them. . . . Get them on the floor and step on them, crush them, show no mercy." When he drew up his enemies list, most of those named were journalists.

Journalists get a charge out of being seen as adversaries. Being on Nixon's enemies list was something they boasted about. One so honored, Mary McGrory, later recalled, "When the list came out, Art Buchwald invited me to lunch at the Sans Souci, and I got a standing ovation." But neither journalists nor their political sources really like being estranged. Politicians need journalists in order to get elected; journalists need politicians in order to have something to write about. Politicians may single out a journalist or two for opprobrium—maybe even freeze them out of interviews for a while. Each side may dine out lavishly after the occasional battle, but both also know you eat regularly if you get along.**

President Kennedy was so miffed about *Time* coverage that he ordered the executive branch not to speak to anyone from the magazine. The ban lasted all of eight hours. It was broken by the president's brother, then attorney general Robert Kennedy, "who talked my ear off," *Time* columnist Hugh Sidey recalled years later.

This mutual dependency is what makes the use of anonymous sources so widespread. It also explains why a 1973 study found that some three-fourths of the stories in the Washington *Post* and the New York *Times* over a twenty-year period involved official sources. And it leads journalists to do what the rest of us do when we want something—cultivate each other. The reporter will buy the politician a drink; the politician will call up a reporter to offer a tip or to have a friendly chat.

---

* President Ford, of course, gave new meaning to the term "presidential trip." A cursory check of news stories from the 1970s found references to nine occasions when Ford stumbled.

** The mutual interests of journalists and news sources are not confined to government. Corporations, for instance, want good news about their products to woo consumers and good news about their financial performance to reassure investors. But the relationship is especially intense in a government that holds regular elections and, as discussed previously, has so many "sunshine" laws.

The results are predictable. "A reporter may hesitate to take a critical view of regularly tapped sources for the very human reason that he prefers to be greeted pleasantly when he walks into an office, rather than to be treated as though he were poison," one veteran Washington reporter has observed. "His vested interest is in maintaining a pleasant atmosphere."

Another Watergate story illustrates how this works. At one point in the investigation of the Nixon White House, Woodward called Secretary of State Henry Kissinger. As the conversation progressed, Kissinger as much as admitted he had authorized wiretaps. Wanting to protect himself, he told Woodward that he wasn't to be quoted. Woodward balked, saying he "could not accept retroactive background." Kissinger fumed. When dealing with reporters who covered the State Department day-to-day, he was accustomed to putting his remarks on ice after he made them. Woodward, however, had never dealt with Kissinger before. The State Department was not his beat, and he didn't care about maintaining a long-term relationship with Kissinger. But the episode did not end there. Kissinger called *Post* editor Ben Bradlee to complain. The story was held for two days, appearing only after it had been broken by the New York *Times*.

Robert Darnton, a New York *Times* reporter turned scholar, observed that "the veteran crime reporters who dominate the press rooms in most police headquarters develop a symbiotic relationship with the police. In Newark there were four tough old reporters who had done more time in headquarters than most of the cops. They knew everyone of importance on the force: they drank with cops, played poker with cops, and adopted the cops' view of crime. They never wrote about police brutality."

In some cases, press cooperation with politicians makes sense. One example is when Boston news organizations worked in 1975 not to inflame a community anguished over a forced school busing plan. On other occasions, particularly during wars, reporters have kept important national security secrets. Three days before dropping the atomic bomb on Hiroshima, President Harry Truman was returning to the United States by ship. He called together the correspondents with him and told them about the top secret device. The journalists, who pledged not to report the conversation, considered the secret "so big and terrifying that we would not discuss it with each other," one reporter later recalled.

To keep reporters from getting too chummy with their sources (for the wrong reasons), editors will move reporters to different beats from time to time, even at the expense of losing the benefit of expertise developed over time.

But many worry this is a lesser problem than the trend of political actors becoming journalists themselves. After the Carter administration, Jody Powell went from White House press secretary to political commentator; Hodding Carter, who was State Department spokesman, returned to journalism; Leslie Gelb, who had left the New York *Times* for policy planning at the State Department, went back to his old paper.

These role reversals give journalists a better understanding of the real pressures of working in government. But not everyone thinks the benefits outweigh the dangers. "Increasingly, foxes are in the chicken coop, and some of us chickens don't like it," veteran political reporter Jules Witcover said.

Even when the lines are clearly marked, though, journalists and politicians can't live without each other. No good reporter fails to report an important bit of news, even if it skewers a prime source. But nose pulling rarely leads to a deadly shoot-out.

## Why Quotes Are (Supposed to Be) Sacred

Of all the tools of American journalism, the "quote" is one of the most favored. Its frequent use sets our press apart from almost any other.

Short for quotation, a quote is the exact phrase spoken or written by another person. At least, it is supposed to be. Tampering with a quote is a professional mortal sin, although one might think otherwise judging from frequent complaints that "I was misquoted."

Until portable tape recorders came along, the sin of misquoting was hard to prove. Nowadays, like two gunslingers at the OK Corral, a reporter and an interviewee will each appear armed with a tape recorder. One is trying to get as many quotes as possible; the other is trying to guard against inaccuracy.

European journalists tend to be disdainful of the American obsession with attribution of facts, including precise quotes. The Europeans (with the exception of the British) hardly bother even taking notes. They insist that the reader only needs to be given the "sense" of what the speaker says. But in the information-heavy system of reporting that has been practiced in the United States for the last half-century, quotes lend verisimilitude to a story. By quoting someone else, you are showing the reader that you, the reporter, are not giving your opinion; someone else is, often in words that are more interesting than anything you could write as a neutral reporter.

Despite the sacredness of quotes, repeating what someone said is harder than it sounds and is not always practiced to the letter. It often is necessary to cleanse and smooth out the inevitable glitches in the spoken phrase—that unnecessary "uh" and "ah" or the wrong verb tense. Sometimes reporters want to capture the flavor of a colorfully expressed phrase and will preserve syntax or grammar errors. But generally they try not to embarrass speakers.

Because of acute sensitivity about being misquoted or misunderstood, some sources demand the interviewer let them review their quotes before publication as a condition for granting an interview. This leads to changes in the original phrasing. "Quote approval is the latest twist in the art of getting someone to talk," noted media critic Philip Weiss. While admitting he sometimes agrees to the practice, Weiss called it "a form of low-level corruption that both parties accept but don't talk about." The reason journalists feel queasy about it is that they give a source the power to manipulate both them and the truth in the interest of making themselves look good.

There's another reason exact quotes are elusive, but this is also a subject seldom talked about: professional shortcomings. Some reporters simply cannot take notes fast enough. American journalists are not required to learn shorthand. Consequently, they often cannot keep up with a rapidly spoken speech.

Most American reporters develop their own homemade system of speed-writing they invariably claim is reliable. But if they are assigned to cover a major speech, they usually depend on either a tape recorder or an advance text provided by the speaker. Reporters tend to be very aggressive in demanding advance copies of speeches from politicians and other newsmakers, who also find advance texts to be good protection against misquoting. If advance copies are not available, the press often waits for the official transcript before writing the story.[*]

---

[*] Because there was no such system used at the time, there are at least two versions of the Gettysburg Address: the one recorded by reporters on the scene and the one given to the press after President Lincoln had a chance to make a few postspeech refinements.

The rules for quoting a public speech leave little room to maneuver for either the journalist or the speaker. If a major and obvious mistake is made in a public speech, the reporter has just two options: quote the speaker exactly, with the caveat [*sic*],* or paraphrase what was said. Major surgery is not allowed. After all, everyone heard it that way.

## Why Sources Can't Clear Stories

If accuracy is so important to journalists, shouldn't they show stories to sources before they are printed? Wouldn't such a procedure help ensure that reporters have their facts straight?

Some journalists do favor the practice of letting the subjects of stories preview them. Not only does this promote accuracy, they say, it also raises credibility with sources, who realize the journalist is dedicated to getting the story right.

Nevertheless, the common sentiment is decidedly against giving sources editorial input after the story is written and before it is published. The fundamental stated reason for this "no show" policy is journalists' bedrock belief in independence. Striving to be objective outsiders, they want to keep the subjects of the news at a safe distance. Behind that feeling, though, are historical, self-interested, and practical factors that shape this bias against prepublication review.

American journalists have fought hard against censorship and its handmaiden, prepublication review. The courts have supported their argument that prior restraint is generally not constitutional. As the Supreme Court has reasoned, "If it can be said that a threat of criminal or civil sanctions after publication 'chills' speech, prior restraint 'freezes' it." But always protective of their First Amendment rights, journalists remain wary of any intrusion into the editorial process.

Journalists argue that prepublication review could make them more vulnerable in a legal proceeding. Having complained about a story beforehand, the source could argue in court that the newspaper was negligent. Just the threat of legal action could result in self-censorship.

---

*The term *sic* is Latin for "thus, it is so," or literally recorded. Using it comes across as a bit snippety.

Veteran reporter Steven Weinberg takes the opposite point of view. "If a subject is angry enough to make such a threat, that same subject will quite likely sue after publication. . . . Should that occur, I suspect many judges and juries would be impressed by a reporter who was so careful and well-intentioned that he or she conducted a prepublication accuracy check."

Apart from First Amendment concerns, journalists regard showing stories to sources as more trouble than it is worth. They often invest a good deal of time selling stories to editors and shepherding each story through the editing process. Few want another layer of review, which can result in haggling like this:

"Your story should discuss every part of the city budget, not just the cuts."

"I can't, there isn't enough room in the newspaper for all of that. And besides the cuts are the news."

"Well then, you really aren't very accurate, are you?"

However much journalists may hate such a conversation, they sometimes will agree to show sources a story in order to get them to cooperate. And however much reporters may advocate showing stories to sources, they sometimes can't. Working under deadline pressures, they just don't have time.

## Why Anyone Would Admit That to a Reporter

Journalists have their tricks to get people to talk. These range from the relatively harmless application of charm to put an interview subject at ease to the more pernicious practice of sneaking up on someone to snap an embarrassing photo.

A common complaint is that reporters use the tactics of an undercover spy. One journalist recently disguised himself as a priest to get into the hospital room of a legendary British jockey who begged for privacy while recovering from a nasty fall. A reporter for ABC's *Prime-Time Live,* using a hidden minicamera, posed as a meatpacker in a major grocery chain to uncover unsanitary practices.

Some journalists are positively indignant when defending such practices: "The public has a right to know about wrongdoing in high places, and this was the only way to uncover it." Not all agree, however. Most thoughtful journalists realize that these tricks undermine the credibility of the press, which is supposed to find and tell the truth, not obscure it.

Some tricks, of course, might be characterized as naughty rather than dishonest or devious. From years of peering across desks during interviews, an experienced reporter gets pretty good at reading reports upside down. Buttering up secretaries is also a fine art in the reporter's repertoire. Here are some other common tricks of the trade:

• *Ice-breaking an interview* by starting off with pleasant chatter about the family dog or yesterday's football game. The purpose here is to put the interview subject at ease. Now convinced against all previous better judgment that the reporter is a human being, the subject blathers blithely on. ("But the reporter was so nice," the burned subject is heard to say later.)

• *Blind-siding* the interviewee with a pointed question after a flurry of marshmallows. This technique is used to put the subject off stride. The reporter hopes he or she will either drop the information inadvertently or, so taken aback, blurt it out.

• *Bluffing* sources to make them think the reporter knows more than he or she actually does. This trick is commonly used when a reporter has a gut instinct something is true but can't prove it. Here's how it can work: The reporter phones a source to check out the hunch. The source will not confirm or deny, so a second source is called. "I was just talking with Joe about that grand jury indictment . . ." The second source is wary, but the barriers are now breaking down. A third source is called. "I've just been on the phone with Joe and Mirabelle on the grand jury indictment, and I'm getting conflicting dates about when the decision will be handed down." By this time, if indeed there is an indictment looming, the reporter may get it confirmed.

• *Shaping the answers.* Sometimes a reporter can shape an answer by asking a leading question, such as "Don't you think your opponent was unfair in the way he presented your record?" Or even more devious: "What are you going to do about the slanderous statements your opponent made?" Perhaps the source wasn't planning to get drawn into a shoot-out with her opponent, but under such questioning, a confrontation becomes difficult to dodge.

• *Not asking any question at all.* Reporters use silence to get more information out of an interview than normally would be volunteered because they know that people tend to feel uncomfortable unless the conversational void is being filled.

Given all these little devices reporters sometimes use, what is the best defense when being grilled? Ken Metzler, a professor of journalism at the University of Oregon, specializes in advising newsmakers on how to deal with the media. He says the answer is not to avoid journalists. "Talk to them, because refusal fuels rumors and causes inaccuracies as they seek alternative sources. If you've done something awful and want no publicity, call a news conference and confess everything in crushing detail. It will be a one-day story and quickly forgotten," Metzler says. He provides several commandments for the wary interviewee:

- Thou shalt not answer speculative questions;
- Thou shalt not allow the interviewer to lead you astray;
- Thou shalt not lie to a reporter;
- Thou shalt not guess the answer;
- Thou shalt be prepared.

The writing side of the journalistic craft has its own bag of tricks. Basically, they fall into two categories: (1) spinning and (2) CYT—covering your tail. If a reporter believes one source more than another, the more credible source may be given more space and prominence in the story. While this is often acceptable if the journalist is acting on a good deal of knowledge, it is less acceptable to signal a source's credibility by using judgmental adjectives (*i.e., strident, elegant*) or verbs (*i.e., conceded, intoned*). Sharp editors usually catch these. In the second category, reporters learn how to fill "holes" in their information. For example, they might say "It was not known whether . . ."

Here are some examples of tactics almost universally condemned within the profession, except in rare cases:

- *Misrepresenting yourself.* Journalists are supposed to identify themselves as such when working. It's one thing to pick up a juicy piece of gossip during off hours at a bar, but it's quite another to start asking questions without telling people it might end up in the newspaper the next day. The worst offense of this kind is posing as someone else, like a policeman. Reporters who want to work undercover need the approval of senior editors, who must weigh the benefits (how important is this story? is this the only way to get it?) against the costs (what does lying about our identity do to our credibility as truth-tellers?).

- *Threats and blackmail.* This is the tell-me-or-else school of interviewing, and it has as much to do with good journalism as a ten-kiloton warhead at a Fourth of July celebration.

• *Not honestly trying to be fair.* If a reporter doesn't really want to give someone a voice in the paper, the story might say the spokesperson "could not be reached for comment by press time," when, in fact, the reporter only let the phone ring twice.

Don Hewitt, the producer of CBS television's popular investigative program *60 Minutes,* justified dissembling this way in an interview with the Washington *Post:* "If you catch someone violating 'thou shalt not steal' by your 'thou shalt not lie,' that's a pretty good trade-off." But for good journalists, this end-justifies-the-means defense is plain wrong.

..................................................................

## Aside: The Ten Commandments of News

With the best seats at baseball games and a daily opportunity to insult the high and mighty, journalists often seem to be above normal restrictions. But this is not true. Not only are they subject to the Ten Commandments, income tax, and speeding laws; they also labor under their own professional constraints.

An informal code of ethics governs journalists. *Informal* is a key word here. No single uniform code of behavior regulates the profession. Several journalism associations as well as individual newspapers and newspaper groups have their own list of "don'ts." None has the force of law. But they are remarkably similar, signaling at least consensus on right and wrong.

Here are ten things most journalists would say they are not supposed to do:

1. Lie in print or on the air (this also means not using new technology to alter photos)

2. Lie to or threaten a source

3. Report rumors or other unverified information

4. Suppress or omit opinion with which one disagrees

5. Show favoritism or personal bias in one's reporting or writing

6. Misrepresent oneself or use deception to get a story (without having very powerful reasons to do so)

7. Plagiarize words or ideas (journalists can use the words with attribution)

8. Tap or tape telephone conversations without permission

9. Use one's position for personal gain (*e.g.,* accepting gifts from sources)

10.  <u>Do anything that may be construed as a "conflict of interest"</u> (*e.g.,* write political speeches for the candidate being covered in an election)

••••••••••••••••••••••••••••••••••••••••••••••••••••••••••••••••••

## Why Good Journalists Don't Pay for News

One practice that separates the "respectable" mainstream press from the so-called tabloid press is that the former does not pay for news and the latter makes a habit of it.*

This is more a matter of ethics than of economics. When money is involved, sources have a good reason to "sell" information the same way advertisers do, with a bit of hype. When that happens, a newspaper's public reputation as a fair and accurate chronicle is brought into question, undermining its credibility.

This "no pay" sentiment is built on another belief. If news is supposed to be in the public domain, it is, in principle, accessible to those who have the enterprise and wherewithal to obtain it, not just those who can afford it. To journalists who take pride in news gathering, "checkbook journalism" is a repellent concept.

It was not always so. In the days when newspapers were the sole source of daily news and cities had several papers competing for readers, publishers fought hard for "exclusives." Turn-of-the-century press barons such as Hearst and Pulitzer routinely paid huge sums for exclusive rights to sensational stories. In 1911 Pulitzer's *World* paid $10,000 for a stunt pilot to fly nonstop from Albany to New York City. Adolph Ochs' New York *Times* scooped the *World* by chartering a train along the flight route and interviewing the pilot when he landed for gas. Two years earlier, the *Times* financed the North Pole expedition of Admiral Robert E. Peary while the *World* underwrote Frederick Cook's trip.**

---

\* "When tabloids get respectable," says one *National Enquirer* reporter, "they're not tabloids anymore."

\*\* In an even earlier period, newspapers occasionally took an altogether different approach. James Gordon Bennett, the genius behind the New York *Herald,* was said to have run an article attacking someone and then to have sent this note to the victim: "Send twenty dollars and it shall be stopped." Wilbur F. Storey's Chicago *Times* consistently gave negative reviews to plays performed in theaters that did not advertise substantially in his paper.

It wasn't until after World War II that a general standard took hold that disparaged checkbook journalism. By midcentury the frenzied battle for "scoops" had abated somewhat as intracity newspaper competition subsided. Television journalists could get their scoops out first.* Personalized (and eccentric) ownership was giving way to corporate ownership, and the mainstream press cared more now about being trusted than being provocative. Tighter professional standards took hold inside newsrooms. Editors wanted to spend the paper's money to help their own reporters get the news themselves. You don't win prizes by paying for stories.

There was also a demographic cause for this cooling down. In the security-conscious postwar years, middle-class Americans drifted away from the frenetic cities, where newsboys used to shout "Extra" from every corner to make their sales, to the white picket fence in suburbia. Families could now count on getting their morning paper on the doorstep, and publishers could count on a daily sale without the need for screaming headlines.

Although journalists have a general distaste for paying for information, they do make markets for exclusive photos and film. In 1983 the New York *Daily News* purchased the photo of a man jumping from the Empire State Building. The tourist, who took the photo, received more than $4,500. This transaction is acceptable, the argument goes, because credibility is not a factor—the camera doesn't lie (or at least it didn't until computerized photo enhancement came along). Perhaps the best-known example of a modern photographic windfall was Abraham Zapruder's 8-millimeter footage of President Kennedy being shot in Dallas' Dealey Plaza. A tourist in the right place at the right time, Zapruder got $25,000 from *Life* magazine for that sequence, a lot of money in the early sixties.

There's also a subculture of freelance photographers who stalk celebrities and peddle their pictures to tabloids. The Europeans and the infamous paparazzi of Italy dominate this field, much to the chagrin of royal families.

Checkbook journalism is gaining some converts in today's more frenzied marketplace, particularly in television. Some two decades ago *60 Minutes* paid two of Richard Nixon's aides, H. R. Haldeman and G. Gordon Liddy, $25,000 and $15,000, respectively, for the right

---

\* By 1952, 34 percent of American homes, 15 million, had a television.

to interview. This practice is even more commonplace now among the proliferating "tabloid" television news shows.

Some argue that since news media can profit from news, sources should be able to do so as well. If this is still a maverick view among newspaper journalists, it is gaining currency among others who work with the printed word. *Sports Illustrated* and *Redbook* have paid for news exclusives. John Burris, an attorney who represented Rodney King, noted a trend in which money-hungry citizens are pushing to serve on juries in sensational trials because they can make big bucks from interviews or book contracts.

A juror in O. J. Simpson's murder trial was replaced when evidence indicated he might have been writing a book about the media event. But in our political system little prevents a sensation-seeking press from providing a feeding trough for a sensation-hungry public. Prompted by the Simpson trial, California lawmakers passed a "checkbook journalism" law. Under the statute, jurors could not sell their stories, and potential witnesses could not accept money for information for one year after the end of a trial. Judges subsequently struck down both as unconstitutional infringements of First Amendment rights.

# VI

..............................

# Journalists' Traits and Foibles

# Why They Don't Dress for Success

It was quite a sight. Coming down the hall was one of the country's better-known investigative reporters . . . dressed neatly. This was a first. His suit fit. It was clean. His tie was snug around his neck, not at half-mast. We marveled. Then he turned in the other direction. The vent of his suit coat was ripped to within a few inches of his collar.

As the tradition has it, newsrooms have as many smart dressers as professional basketball teams have players under six feet tall. In fact, sloppy dress, and all that is suggested by that, has become a metaphor for journalism. But while the metaphor holds some truth, it is also an exaggeration.

Here are some realities that swirl about journalistic fashion and lifestyles.

• Newspaper reporters are considered sloppy dressers for the same reason Harvard president Charles W. Eliot once described them as "drunkards, deadbeats, and bummers." People see them as chasing after news without much concern for their dignity, social graces, or familial responsibility. Remember Oscar Madison, the sloppy one in *The Odd Couple*? He was a journalist.

No doubt about it, the cycle of daily journalism intensifies the work of editors and reporters. "An editor has a twenty-four-hour window," says Bill Kovach, a former editor of the Atlanta *Constitution*. "You don't have time to think about tomorrow's newspaper." It is not uncommon to find aggressive reporters who seem slightly crazed and perpetually in a hurry, pockets or purses stuffed with pens and paper. Television journalists look in the mirror before they go on camera; newspaper journalists do their stories without makeup.

But forget the idea that newspaper journalists are congenitally unable to live in civilized society after hours—that they work under such stress that they have astronomically high rates of divorce, drink excessively, and are irreligious.

Journalists show the same proclivity for married life as other people, according to a 1989 study by the American Society of Newspaper Editors (ASNE): "More than half (57 percent) of the newsroom work force is married, about the same as the U.S. labor force as a whole (61 percent). . . . A quarter (27 percent) of newsroom workers are single, never married (compared with 25 percent of the U.S. labor force). The rest are divorced (7 percent), widowed (1 percent), or 'involved in a significant relationship' (7 percent)."

What about children? According to the same report, "Sixty-seven percent of the journalists have no children at home, compared with 60 percent of the total work force." But this trend may be changing. "Some 20 percent of the journalists have children under 6 years of age, compared with 18 percent of the national work force."

As for boozing, the trends follow the general direction of society. In the old days reporters—mostly male—may have gone to the local bar for a straight whiskey after meeting their deadlines.* Now, like everybody else, they are more inclined to go home and help make dinner and put the kids to bed. Correspondingly, press clubs, once popular watering holes for journalists, are going the way of all-male newsrooms. Only nineteen existed as of mid-1990, said Harry Bodaan, then general manager of Washington's National Press Club. That, he estimated, was down from about fifty in the early 1980s. The Atlanta Press Club, one of the largest in the country, is a survivor. It doesn't have a bar.

Not only are journalists drinking mineral water along with the rest of the country but they take to church just about the same as their neighbors. More than 80 percent are believers, according to the ASNE study.

• Underlying the sloppy dress image is the notion that journalists don't dress well because they have crummy salaries. Haute fashion

---

*This boozing image creeps into and is perpetuated by literature. Here is a passage from Edwin O'Connor's *The Last Hurrah:* "Tom, let's get the gentlemen of the press in here. They're busy men: they have to hurry back to their papers, write their stories, and get out to the saloons."

along with fancy sports cars and pricey vacations are out of reach. In the words of Jimmy Breslin, the flamboyant *Newsday* columnist, newspaper reporters "aren't good looking enough and have lousy voices for television. They make about one-tenth the money of a television news star and are virtually unknown."

Truth be told, publishers and the top editors often command good salaries these days.* The salaries for reporters, copy editors, and the like are not sensational, but they are not so bad, either. The Bureau of Labor Statistics puts median weekly earnings for reporters and editors at $614 a week, just about in the middle. They are above social workers and police officers, on a par with accountants, and below lawyers. According to another study, the median annual income for all daily newspaper reporters was $35,180 in 1991. Local television journalists' salaries were much lower (the median was $25,625). At *Newsday* reporters are wearing striped shirts, suspenders, or designer suits.

But Breslin, for all his exaggerating, is not altogether wrong about television. He understands that the big names in TV news—even big local names—earn much more than star newspaper journalists. Big-time television journalists have agents. Newspaper journalists generally don't—unless they also appear regularly on television talk shows. Then they also get large fees for speaking.**

• Journalists dress poorly, it is also suggested, because they don't want to be in fashion. They fancy themselves outsiders, detached. Relishing that role, New York *Times* reporter George Vecsey described Michael Jordan as "wearing a suit so elegant, so expensive-looking that a scruffy sports reporter could not begin to describe it."

According to this argument, journalists like to signal their distrust of everything; they're not joiners. The ASNE study showed, however, that 59 percent characterized themselves as being involved in community affairs as much as or more than "other people my age."

---

* The *Media Industry Newsletter* reported these salaries in 1994: Iain Calder, editor of the *National Enquirer,* $631,000; Burl Osborne, Dallas *Morning News* publisher, $919,000; Arthur Sulzberger, Jr., New York *Times* publisher, $587,000.

** As reported in the *Wall Street Journal* April 15, 1994, panelists on television talk shows not only become attractive as speakers but also can command higher prices. One executive with a speakers' bureau noted that a panelist on a talk show will receive up to $5,000 for a speech and a moderator $10,000.

Even the 41 percent who don't participate as much as their peers are not really nonconformist. Journalists may not wear Armani suits, but they don't wear Hare Krishna robes, either.

## Why They Are Reformers, Not Revolutionaries

When Spiro Agnew, Richard Nixon's vice-president, called journalists "nattering nabobs of negativism," the public knew what he meant: Journalists are destructive. They tear down institutions and people. Journalists may not have liked Agnew's comments, but they fuel such feelings. They like the image of themselves ramming the portals of government.

Political rhetoric and self-congratulations aside, there is some truth in the press's antiestablishment image. They report the failure of cherished institutions. They are cynical about the people they cover. But they are not about to mount an insurrection. They believe in the system and want to improve it. Reformers they may be. But revolutionaries they definitely are not.

Consider the demographics. Revolutionaries typically come from the ranks of the very poor or the very wealthy. But journalists, whether from newspapers, magazines, or television, are decidedly from the American middle class. More than 90 percent are white; about half are male and half are Protestant. Pay, as noted in the previous section, will let a journalist keep up with the Joneses but not move far ahead.

As the quotable publisher E. W. Scripps once noted, "I have only one principle, and that is represented by an effort to make it harder for the rich to grow richer and easier for the poor to keep from growing poorer." At first glance he may have sounded like someone intent on redistributing wealth. As much as anything, though, he was reflecting a common newspaper orientation favoring a strong middle class.*

While journalists may not be inclined to tear down the fundamental structures of American society, they have an inclination to see it improved. Those attracted to journalism tend to be idealists with ro-

---

* Scripps certainly had no interest in giving his own wealth away; at one point he required reporters to pay their own carfare to cover stories and to buy their own pencils.

mantic views of their jobs and the world. Journalists are the kind of people who in college disliked business courses and gravitated toward the humanities. Journalism degrees require students to take three-fourths of their courses in the liberal arts. And those young people who come to the profession without journalism degrees generally come with degrees in some liberal arts subject, such as English, history, or political science. Only 2.3 percent of journalists with college degrees major in business administration; 0.3 percent major in mathematics; 1.6 percent major in physical or biological sciences.*

Quite often reform-minded journalists have inspired young people to follow in their footsteps. Star journalists from an earlier generation read the autobiography of Lincoln Steffens, one of the great "muckrakers." The aggressive investigative reporting of the 1960s and 1970s coincided with new highs in journalism school enrollments. Would-be journalists got their inspiration from the Watergate book and movie *All the President's Men.*

Some of this romanticism may burn off as journalists grow older. But the front lines of journalism are dominated by the youngest members of the profession, the reporters. What's more, the culture of journalism nurtures romantic feelings even among editors. Editors are honored by their peers for supporting reform-minded reporters, not shutting them down.

This altruism reveals itself when surveys measure journalists' job satisfaction. Having seen their pay decline relative to comparable professions like accounting and auditing, newspaper reporters might be expected to put money higher on wish lists. But in an early 1980s study, 61 percent of the journalists surveyed ranked "helping people" very important while only 23 percent ranked "pay" very important. Fifty-seven percent ranked "job security" and "editorial policy" as very important. A more recent study, commissioned by the Associated Press Managing Editors Association, had similar findings. Reporters wanted attentive managers and a chance for promotions and intellectual growth. Job satisfaction correlated closely to the quality of the newspaper; compensation was less important.

---

* This doesn't mean that journalists are terrible at math, just that they are more attuned to the written word. Journalism students taking the Scholastic Assessment Test score at the national average for math and higher than the national average on verbal parts of the test.

The ASNE study cited earlier concluded that one of the most important things managers of newsrooms can do for staff morale and retention is "stay true to the primary First Amendment functions of the press. The newspaper's responsibilities to the public and the American system are very important to the newsroom staff."

Journalists usually don't declare their political affiliations, but surveys show them as a group to be left of center: 44 percent consider themselves Democrats, 16 percent Republican, and 34 percent independent. Other recent surveys bear this out. The Media Leadership Forum reported in 1995 that 85 percent of media leaders polled agreed the media tends to be more liberal than American voters. A Times Mirror study that same year found "the public is significantly more conservative than the media." On social issues the media appeared particularly tolerant. More than four out of five local and national print journalists felt that homosexuality should be accepted by society. Other polls have shown them more open than the general public to foreign aid and abortion.

But put the accent on center, not left. These are not bomb throwers. Those who tend toward liberalism don't go far to the left. The Times Mirror poll found only 2 percent classified themselves as "very liberal." And many classify themselves as moderate. Overall, journalists prefer to congregate around the center, and they take more pride in being neutral than being part of a party. Some, like the editor of the Akron *Beacon-Journal,* don't even vote for fear they will be seen as taking sides. Not taking sides, of course, is to vote more or less for the status quo.

. . . . . . . . . . . . . . . . . . . . . . . . . . . . . . . . . . . . . . . . . . . . . . . . . . . . . . . . . . . . . . . .

## Aside: Ten Comments That Will Irritate a Reporter

1. *Your paper lies.*

In 1835 a New York *Sun* reporter wrote a series of stories describing "discoveries" of life on the moon, including the existence of man-bat creatures. The public was good-natured about the hoax, but today the accent in the workplace is on "being professional." In the case of journalists, that means either telling the truth or getting the boot.

2. *Your paper is biased.*

Bias suggests motive, and journalists like to think they have no motive but to seek the truth. To charges of bias they have a lot of pat answers, which go something like this: "Half our readers think we are too liberal and half think we are too conservative; we must be doing something right."

3. *You misquoted me.*

This implies the journalist can't take proper notes or, worse, slants quotes to fit ulterior motives. When hearing this complaint, the reporter suspects that sources wish they had kept their mouths shut and now want to duck blame.

4. *When I saw the headline, I didn't read any further.*

Reporters hate taking the rap for a misleading headline, which they didn't write and which, in their minds, oversimplifies a wonderful piece of journalism.

5. *You just want to sell newspapers.*

The charge is wrong. Reporters aren't working to sell newspapers; they're trying to write stories that get their byline on the front page. That's how they advance their careers.

6. *We need you to get the word out.*

Journalists are forever fending off attempts by people with vested interests to use the press for their own purposes. They don't like the idea of being used, even for a good cause.

7. *Where's your sense of patriotism?*

Journalists see their profession as the ultimate public service. They feel embattled by this question. From their point of view, questioning government is a patriotic act.

8. *Why didn't you guys publish my letter?*

The reporter doesn't have the faintest idea what happened to this letter.

9. *You didn't let the facts get in the way of a good story.*

The classic insider statement of this is from columnist Diana McLellan: "Never check stories out, dear. That's how you lose them." When said by a reader who is trying to goad the journalist, the journalist blushes or bristles. This is the worst of all charges, making up news instead of sticking to facts.

10. *You never admit when you're wrong.*

Being wrong in itself hurts, but refusing to admit when you're wrong implies cowardice and arrogance. Corrections rarely, if ever, occurred in the past. A newspaper simply stonewalled until threatened with a lawsuit. Today "clarifications" appear frequently in order to demonstrate that the Fourth Estate is self-policing. But journalists still find a way to avoid responsibility with phrases like "Due to a computer error," "Due to erroneous information," and "Due to the solar eclipse."

••••••••••••••••••••••••••••••••••••••••••••••••••••••••••••••••••••••••••

## Why They Pick on People

> In the old days men had the rack. Now they have the press. That is an improvement, certainly. But still it is very bad, and wrong, and demoralizing.
>
> —Oscar Wilde, 1892

The press badgered Jimmy Carter when he claimed to have fended off a "killer rabbit" that swam toward him with teeth bared while he was canoeing in a swamp.* It hounded vice-presidential candidate Geraldine Ferraro over apparent irregularities in her tax returns, her financial statements as a member of Congress, and her husband's business records. It mocked Vice-President Dan Quayle for misspelling *potato.* It never gets enough of Charles and Diana, who do their part by whispering to their lovers on car phones. There are times when the great champion of the "people's right to know" comes across as little more than a bully. Washington journalists collectively wrote off Bill Clinton's presidency within six months of his inauguration, elevated him to near hero stature two years later, and declared him a terminal case a year after that.

It seems that once journalists smell blood, they attack en masse, not letting up until the subject is picked clean. Presidential misstatements are especially mouthwatering. During the height of the cold war, Gerald Ford once said, "There is no Soviet domination of Eastern Europe, and there never will be under a Ford administration." After several similarly inaccurate statements, reporter David Broder noted, "An image had been fixed in the minds of the reporters covering Ford and it was sustained by them with whatever material came to hand."

Carter, expressing a common feeling among politicians, complained that journalists don't want better explanations of policies;

---

* Episodes like this live on for years. A search of the Nexis database of 1994 news stories turned up twenty-five references to the "killer rabbit"—this eighteen years after the attack.

they want "a radical, distorted, unprecedented comment," even if it is taken out of context.

Politicians, of course, are not the only targets of media blitzes, and the phenomenon is neither new nor always focused on matters as trivial as rabbit attacks. One of the more infamous cases took place in the 1930s when the press latched onto the kidnapping and murder of Charles Lindburgh's baby. Scenes of screaming and shoving reporters, blaring headlines based on flimsy rumor, and total disregard of the famous aviator's privacy caused mass public revulsion. Some say that this hysterical coverage (in excess of three hundred reporters who wired more than eleven million words) also created a "trial by newspaper," violating suspect Bruno Hauptmann's right to a fair hearing.

Why do journalists sometimes behave this way? Larry Sabato, a professor of government at the University of Virginia, devoted a book, *Feeding Frenzy,* to examining the problem, its causes, and possible remedies. One thing that is *not* a cause, Sabato says, is a press "conspiracy," at least in the classic sense of a plot. Editors and reporters don't get on the phone with each other and say, "Let's go after this guy." After all, the media in this country are intensely competitive (as well as too disorganized to launch any meaningful, monolithic campaign). But ironically, it is just this competition that willy-nilly brings journalists together and creates the impression of collusion. When a hot story breaks, news organizations tend to move in the same direction. No one wants to be accused of falling behind a rival in covering the story. Thus, fear is a major motivating force for pack journalism.

In recent years, Sabato says, press guilt over past failures also has driven journalists to excessive zeal. As he explains it, the American press today is chastising itself for once looking the other way at political misbehavior, particularly in regard to the "character" issue. Franklin D. Roosevelt, John F. Kennedy, and many other American political figures had personal foibles and committed indiscretions that the press knew about but never reported. Journalists were part of the Washington "club" and avoided informing on its members.

Media watchers tie this increased aggression to a number of events that discredited people in power: Senator Edward Kennedy driving his car into the water off Chappaquiddick Island and drowning Mary Jo Kopechne; Watergate and especially the White House transcripts, which stripped the mystique off the office of the chief executive; Jimmy Carter promoting character as a criterion for the presidential leadership. The women's movement also has played a role by putting household matters and family relationships on the public radar screen.

Nixon played a special role in this transformation for reasons that went beyond Watergate. His handlers perfected techniques for shaping presidential image. Realizing this, journalists along with much of the public became more cynical about those in power. "The reporter used to gain status by dining with his subjects," Adam Gopnik notes. "Now he gains status by dining on them." As Sabato puts it, the media went from "lapdog" to "watchdog" to "junkyard dog."

Preoccupation with character in politics has a strong ethical premise. The press sees itself obligated to inform the public about personal behavior that could seriously influence public action. Revelations about Oregon senator Robert Packwood's behavior toward female staffers are examples of what the media (and the public) generally regard as a true public service.

The high ground starts crumbling, however, when the subject matter is petty and the information is flimsy or distorted. This often happens when journalists get fixated on a behavioral stereotype and search out examples to reinforce it—*i.e.,* Ford is a "bumbler," Carter is "spineless," Quayle is "stupid."

In today's tell-all climate, even the so-called serious press, which would prefer to stay above the unseemly fray, finds itself being sucked in. The first report of Bill Clinton's extramarital affairs with Gennifer Flowers came in the *Star.* The *Globe,* another sensational tabloid, was the first to report the alleged rape of a woman by William Kennedy Smith. In both cases, establishment network and newspaper journalists followed. "What now is the press to do . . . in an environment in which a whole culture has undergone tabloidization?" asked Los Angeles *Times* reporter Tom Rosenstiel in his book, *Strange Bedfellows: How Television and the Presidential Candidates Changed Presidential Politics.*

As a remedy for the worst excesses of attack journalism, Sabato has proposed what he calls a "fairness doctrine" that would be acceptable to the press, politicians, and public. Basically, the doctrine calls for restraint in reporting personal behavior that is not regarded as serious or compulsive enough to affect an official's public duty; the press is also cautioned to avoid reporting about the irrelevant activities of a politician's family, especially underage children.

If past history is any guide, policies such as this will not produce much result. Journalists often chastise themselves for pack journalism, but the collective *mea culpas* are themselves a sign of the bonds that come from competitive instincts.

# Why They Are So Pushy

Journalism is not a career for the reticent. Reporters quickly learn they must shove their way to the front of the crowd. This requires sensible shoes and what New Yorkers call "moxie"—a Yiddish word for courage with a hint of aggression. The shrinking violets either end up on the overnight desk or learn to exploit their shyness to disarm unwary sources with tough questions.

This pushiness takes different forms.

• In *Slaughterhouse-Five,* Kurt Vonnegut ruefully related his experience as a young reporter in Chicago covering the gruesome death of a man crushed in an elevator accident. An editor told him to break the news to the man's wife and get a reaction. Almost every journalist can relate a similar experience.

• Interviews can be cordial, but always around the corner is the need to probe beyond what the source wants to say. ABC reporter Sam Donaldson's badgering tone in White House press conferences is extreme but not out of character for the profession.

• When President Kennedy was shot in Dallas in 1963, Jack Bell of AP and Merriman Smith of UPI were in a car behind him. Smith grabbed the only phone in the car and wouldn't let go even after Bell took a swing at him. UPI relayed worldwide the first news of the shots. Smith won a Pulitzer Prize for his coverage of the assassination.

A host of factors contribute to this aggression. One of them is frequent exposure to the dark side of life. "I have found journalism to be an endless struggle with the forces of greed, lust, violence and ignorance, all of which continue to have the upper hand," Donald Skinner, twenty-year veteran, wrote on the day he retired from the Orange County, California, *Register.*

Add to this the gnawing anxiety of having to meet a daily deadline and the sense of entitlement, power, and self-righteousness that comes with carrying a press pass, that little laminated identification card that says, "Let me in." The Cable News Network's Frank Sesno describes the industrial-strength Attitude that comes with this heady mix: "How dare they not come clean? How dare they not tell the full story? What are they trying to hide? Why are they hiding it? . . . Goddammit, you're going to get the truth!"

Television has accentuated journalists' aggression. When Newt Gingrich transformed the House Speaker's traditionally civil news conferences by opening them to cameras, print journalists became more hostile. Hoping to get on the evening TV news themselves, New York *Times* reporter Adam Clymer observed, journalists asked confrontational questions likely to draw a highly newsworthy response. Gingrich reacted by cutting back on these media meetings and looking for opportunities when he would be in more control.

Getting on the tube may satisfy a journalist's ego, but it also makes journalists' pushiness more obvious to the public. Americans have become disenchanted with what they see as gross media arrogance. When Dan Rather jauntily challenged Richard Nixon at a White House press conference during the Watergate scandal, angry letters poured into CBS demanding to know how a reporter would dare speak to the president of the United States with such disrespect. Because most journalists like to think they are representing the public's interests, this lack of appreciation can be galling. Like overworked police, they tend to develop a siege mentality and find themselves only enjoying each other's company.

Occasionally one meets a journalist who contradicts the stereotype. Gene Roberts, the legendary Philadelphia editor who in 1994 was coaxed out of a teaching job to become managing editor of the New York *Times,* seems to be the antithesis of the arrogant and aggressive journalist—soft-spoken, tentative and pensive, painfully awkward in a crowd. Those qualities can be misleading, however. As many an underling and newsmaker has learned too late, Roberts took advantage of his image as a mole squinting silently from the sidelines. He was either ignored or trusted just when he wanted to be. In the process, he often managed to pry out better stories than the shouters and the swaggerers in the front row.*

---

* In addition to receiving many kudos for his reporting, Roberts led the Philadelphia *Inquirer* to seventeen Pulitzer Prizes as executive editor. Harrison Salisbury called him "simply the best journalist living and breathing in the U.S.A., and probably the world."

•••••••••••••••••••••••••••••••••••••••••••••••••••••••••••••••••••

### Aside: Other Peculiar Habits of the Press

• *"How do you feel . . . ?"* With the advent of television news and its spotlight on reporters at work, this lead-in has become enshrined as a monument to insensitive journalism. It usually precedes a question to the grief-stricken about the untimely death of a loved one. Amazingly, reporters are still asking questions like this (although many won't anymore). Why does it persist? The short answer is *human interest.* As macabre and distasteful as it may seem, journalists are convinced that the public finds the expression of extreme emotion, such as grief and anger, to be riveting news.

• *The obsession with secrets.* If information is power, secret information is extra power, and that extra power has an irresistible appeal to a certain breed of journalist. It may seem a contradiction for journalists to harbor secrets when they spend so much time exposing others for doing so. But some who stalk the corridors of power have a great compulsion to "be in the know," to have that private bit of information that no one else has. In this regard, journalism has a kinship to espionage. Indeed, a fascination with spying may help account for all those breathless books journalists wrote about CIA traitor Aldrich Ames (four published in 1995 alone).

• *We did that story last year.* In an episodic environment dominated by the quest for newness, the press has an aversion to repeating itself, unless it is consciously keeping a hot story alive—like the O. J. Simpson trial. But when it comes to making a repeat visit to a story, even one affecting an enormous number of people, editors waver. So, for example, if a foreign correspondent messages the front office that he wants to visit Uganda to do a story on how that African nation's recovery program is going, he could well get the reply: "Forget it, we did Uganda last year." The public's tolerance for "old-hat" news is not nearly as low as that of those who gather it.

•••••••••••••••••••••••••••••••••••••••••••••••••••••••••••••••••••

# Why They Give Themselves Prizes

Here's the top news in one of those what-we-did-this-year letters mass-circulated to friends around Christmas time: Poor Jim, the letter said, "missed getting the big one by a hair." Jim is a journalist. The "big one" required no explanation.

Even the greenest rookie knows the "big one" is the Pulitzer Prize, the MVP of American journalism. Named for and by Joseph Pulitzer, one of the leading sensational journalists in the late nineteenth century, Pulitzers are given annually for a variety of exemplary journalism feats, from investigative and foreign reporting to editorial writing. Publishers covet it; editors measure their prowess by it; reporters die for it—and if they live to receive the award in person, it is sure to be highlighted in their obituary when they do pass away. But what does it all mean for the newspaper reader?

Many in the journalistic fraternity are quick to say that such recognition, particularly by one's peers, provides a benchmark for excellence, a spotlight on the highest standards of public service, and a goal for young professionals. But not everyone in the fraternity agrees. H. L. Mencken, a journalist as well as a satirist, called the Pulitzers "imbecilities repeated annually." He regarded them as inappropriate, boastful, and irrelevant.

In theory, a news story or column that is worthy of a prize is one that also benefits the readers, by exposing corruption in high places, alerting the public to a major health hazard, exploring the unknown, explaining a complicated policy, or campaigning to right an injustice. But Mencken's objection had more to do with motive than content. Was that long-winded series on tax loopholes, splashed across the front page for a week, primarily meant for the reader or for an awards jury? Was the reason for launching a major investigation one of public service or professional ego?

Prize giving is not confined to the Pulitzer. More than five hundred nationally advertised prizes are offered each year to American journalists and news organizations. The prizes reward excellence in coverage of almost every conceivable subject—the environment, health, education, business, agriculture, and such specific topics as the retail garment industry or women's sports. There are awards for courage, ethics, zeal, feature writing, newspaper design, and photography. There's an award for coverage of Unidentified Flying Objects (UFOs) and for "presentation of biblical truth in a sensitive, thought-provoking manner." And don't overlook the American Penal Press Contest, the Colonel William L. Lookadoo Photojournalism Awards, and the Non-Heatset Printing Awards Contest.

Those are just national awards. Every state has its own set of awards, often sponsored by the local press association or journalism school but also by other interested parties. The "other interested parties," both locally and nationally, might also be described as "special interests": banks, the insurance industry, medical associations, and other institutions that journalists are supposed to cover with cold-eyed objectivity.

Can journalists be impartial if they accept prizes from these news-makers? As editor of the Philadelphia *Inquirer,* Gene Roberts took his reporters out of the prestigious contest for financial reporting run by the Amos Tuck School at Dartmouth College. Although that business school remained involved in the awards program, the name of the award had been changed to the Champion Media Awards for Economic Understanding—Champion as in the Champion Paper Products Company. "Of concern to me is what I perceive to be the beginning of a trend to use awards to promote corporate names," Roberts said.

News organizations generally initiate the award process themselves with an application to the sponsor that often includes an entry fee. Large papers, such as the Miami *Herald* and the Los Angeles *Times,* have staff members who do little else but compile attractive submissions. At smaller papers, PR firms are sometimes employed to put together entries. "If you've ever served on one of those award juries, with the hundreds of pages you have to wade through, it makes a big difference if the material is clean and looks sharp," says Richard Cooper, deputy Washington bureau chief for the Los Angeles *Times.*

One reason the Pulitzer is so coveted is that it is granted by the most important editors in the United States, who sit on a board convened by Columbia University. Peer recognition is not only highly valued by professionals but avoids, in theory at least, the conflict-of-interest problem created by outside sponsors. In practice, another kind of conflict arises when many of the awards go to newspapers whose editors serve on the selection board.

Being judged by one's peers is fine if that's a true gauge of excellence for a newspaper, but does this focus the newspaper on its most important audience, the hometown reader? According to Rich Oppel, former Washington bureau chief for the Knight-Ridder newspaper chain, contests force newspapers "to start thinking about how some editor in Des Moines is going to view our work."

Whether the profusion of journalism awards is more harmful than beneficial will continue to be debated. A good case can be made for prizes motivating journalists to excel. But even those who are cynical about awards don't expect such laurels to disappear. After all, even though Mencken didn't think much of them, at least two awards are given annually in his name.

## Why They Want Their Names in Print

Reporters come to stories with particular backgrounds, personalities, prejudices, and ambitions. By placing the author's name, or byline, over an article, the newspaper acknowledges the subjective nature of journalism. It is saying: This is not a monolithic institution, but a reflection of our diversity.

Of course, this is not the only reason for bylines. They are also a cheap reward system. And they allow management to instill a greater sense of responsibility in a reporter. After all, if the story contains an error, everyone knows whom to blame.*

Uncle Sam ushered in the modern tradition of bylines. During the Civil War, the Union War Department insisted that reporters sign or initial their dispatches so it could hold them accountable for the accuracy and impact of their stories. With the public following war news so avidly, newspapers learned the value of carrying bylines of their favored writers, especially when they wrote first-person accounts of their heroic exploits in getting the story.

But until the mid-twentieth century, most writers remained soldiers in an anonymous legion. According to purists, readers weren't supposed to know or care who wrote a story. It was the news itself that counted.

In addition to not being recognized in those early days, reporters were not paid very well, either. Their main compensation was the thrill of "newspapering" and the freebies that came with the job. They

---

*Taking the heat off the newspaper is a related effect of bylines, says media historian Michael Emery, "but not necessarily a motive." He notes the case of Paul Conrad, political cartoonist for the Los Angeles *Times*. His work during the Palestinian uprising in the early 1990s greatly upset the local Jewish community. "They dumped garbage on Conrad's lawn, not on the Los Angeles *Times*."

often got free meals, drinks, rides, and tickets to the ballgame. They did creative things with company expense accounts. But in the 1950s, higher profits and the growth of unionism helped to propel journalists to middle-class status and, in turn, to require more professional behavior. With this, and the realization that bylines were an inexpensive way of maintaining the morale of an ambitious and largely egocentric staff, employers gradually took off the veil of anonymity. It didn't hurt that bylines made the newspaper seem a little less impersonal.

The *Times-Picayune* in New Orleans is representative of the shift toward more byline credit. On a date chosen at random—Friday, April 8, 1920—it ran fourteen front-page stories. None carried a byline. On April 7, 1995, also a Friday, it ran five front-page stories, all of which had bylines.

News magazines proved more resistant to the personalization of the press. Bylines only began appearing as tags on major stories in *Newsweek* in 1975 and in *Time* in 1980. A strong force pushing all print media to give reportorial credit has been television. Television encourages personalities to emerge, even those of the reporters. They not only end on-air reports by giving their names but the viewers hear their voices and see their faces.* Television also has made print reporters into what are commonly called "celebrity journalists." David Broder, George Will, and Eleanor Clift are more recognizable than many of the people they cover.

Giving credit is so much the rule today that bylines are considered a reporter's right, even for minor stories. If a small community newspaper has only a handful of reporters, it is not unusual to see the same byline over three or four stories, sometimes on the same page.

"We've become prisoners of the system," says a weekly newspaper editor in Virginia, shaking his head.

Says Thomas Winship, former editor of the Boston *Globe,* "Twenty-five years ago you had to earn a byline. Today reporters put their own names on the story without asking."

---

* Of course, the biggest television personalities—the anchors—rarely gather or write news. That is done by behind-the-scenes journalists, who get no credit. CBS anchor Dan Rather didn't even write his autobiographies, *The Camera Never Blinks* and *The Camera Never Blinks Twice;* he used a ghostwriter.

# VII

## The Public and the Press

# Why the Watchdog Hates to Be Watched

Journalists take great pride in their role as watchdogs fearlessly guarding the commonweal. Yet, when it comes time to consider how *they* should be watched, they protest. At a Columbia University forum in 1992, television reporter Garrick Utley summed up the traditional journalistic sentiment: Everyone's business is a journalist's business, and a journalist's business is no one's business.

Journalists become outraged whenever it appears that someone is hemming them in. They want to know where and how much legislators earn in speaking fees, but don't want anyone looking at their own finances, even if their outside income might show their own ties to special interests. In campaigning for a seat on the Standing Committee of Correspondents, which governs the congressional press galleries, John Harwood of the *Wall Street Journal* called for journalists seeking gallery credentials to disclose outside income. He lost. Shortly afterward in 1995, West Virginia senator Robert Byrd proposed legislation calling for the same thing. "Offensive and insulting," said the president of the Society of Professional Journalists.

Senator Byrd's proposal, tantamount to media licensing, is probably unconstitutional. But this still leaves open a thorny question, "Who guards the guardians?"

Consider the difficulties of starting independent bodies to review public complaints about news coverage. The idea of news councils surfaced as early as the 1930s but went nowhere. In 1947 the proposal came again in a highly publicized report by the Commission on Freedom of the Press established by *Time* publisher Henry R. Luce. The group was chaired by University of Chicago president Robert M. Hutchins and included poet Archibald MacLeish and

theologian Reinhold Niebuhr—and no journalists. Foreshadowing
how the media would regard organized criticism, Luce rejected the
Hutchins commission's findings, deriding them for an "appalling lack
of even high school logic." With similar sentiments expressed by
other media leaders, the council idea went nowhere until the late
1960s, when it was tested on the local level. Not until 1973 was a
National News Council established, with eight journalists and ten
public members.

None of these efforts fared well. The National News Council shut
down in 1984, hampered by lack of support from the media. The only
local effort of any note, the Minnesota News Council, struggles along.

Of the 1,253 complaints directed to it, the National News Council
took no action on 199, dismissed 827 without a formal hearing, and
made a full determination on 227. Here are some typical cases, as described by the council:

• "Was an article in *New York* magazine an unfounded attack on
voluntary child-care services and the state of foster care?"

• "In 1972, one of the nation's largest wood-products firms had a
severe financial setback. Did a United Press International story mis-
leadingly imply that the company was covering up its past?"

• "Was a Quad-City *Times* story on a fifteen-year-old murder suspect in the public interest, or did it jeopardize the teenager's right to
a fair trial?"

• "When a former president of the Allegheny County Bar Association in Pennsylvania was proposed as a candidate for a federal judge-
ship, a Pittsburgh television station broadcast an investigative report
about her business associations that questioned her fitness to serve in
the post. Was the report fair?"

In each case the National News Council issued a report, stating the
question, providing background, and giving its verdict along with the
vote of each council member. Dissenting opinions also were noted. A
newspaper's compliance was voluntary. It could publish the findings
or issue a correction if it were in the wrong—or ignore the reports
entirely. There were no fines or other sanctions for errant journalists
or their newspapers, magazines, or broadcast stations.

A Twentieth-Century Fund Task Force, which established the
National News Council, correctly predicted that "editors and publishers may fear that a media council will stimulate public hostility; some
even maintain that it might curtail rather than preserve their freedom." Journalists argued that news councils could open the door for

stronger restrictions and might be used in court decisions against newspapers.

Unofficial review by an outside agent could give the public greater confidence that journalists are not an unchecked force. Active news councils could reduce the amount of news-related court cases, and a little unofficial monitoring could save them from what they fear most: government oversight. Yet the majority of newspapers and professional press associations continue to shun the idea. When the Louisville *Courier-Journal* proposed a state news council to be funded by the legislature and run by the journalism department at the University of Kentucky, most of the state's newspapers and the Kentucky Press Association joined in opposition. After initially showing interest in the proposal, the Bluegrass State's legislature voted it down in March, 1994.

A more limited approach to checking the transgressions of newspapers—and giving the public a vehicle for voicing objections—has been the use of ombudsmen. Ombudsmen serve as internal critics and points of contact for outsiders who feel they have not been treated properly. The Scandinavians pioneered the concept in the early nineteenth century as a way to monitor government bureaucracy and handle citizen grievances. Applying the concept to newspapers received considerable attention in 1967 with articles by press critic Ben Bagdikian in *Esquire* and by New York *Times* editor A. H. Raskin in his paper. The Times did not develop a "Department of Internal Criticism," as Raskin suggested, but the Louisville *Courier-Journal* picked up on the idea and in 1964 became the first to try it. Its ombudsman wrote a daily appraisal of the paper for editors and handled reader complaints. Not long after that the Washington *Post* created an ombudsman position, adding to its duties the writing of a column on the editorial page. As of 1995 the Organization of News Ombudsmen would fit into a modest meeting room. It has forty-two members. About 97 percent of U.S. and Canadian newspapers quite happily do without.

Ombudsmen provide the public with a link to the paper. The problem is that ombudsmen are hired and paid by the newspaper, an awkward position for even the most tough-minded individual. "They never got the *Post* out of me," Richard Harwood reflected on his two stints as Washington *Post* ombudsman, "and I suspect most ombudsmen are like that, appointed to the job after years of association with the institutions toward which they are now expected to become neutral and disinterested. . . . The editors and reporters are old pals. The publisher has buttered our bread." Bagdikian, the *Post*'s second ombudsman, had no compunction about annoying his bosses. Among other things, he wrote that "blacks could use a boycott as one means to force newspapers to give coverage of black communities." He was fired after eleven months.

Many journalists say the press has no business covering itself. It simply can't be objective and, anyway, the media is not a public concern. Some journalists have gone so far as to object to press reviews, the two most prominent being the *American Journalism Review* and the *Columbia Journalism Review.* While this is a strong opinion not widely shared, journalism reviews have had a struggle to survive and are rarely read by the general public.

In an effort to boost sagging credibility with the public, newspapers have been more willing to print corrections, publish expanded letters-to-the-editor sections, and assign reporters to news stories about the news business. More often newspapers put citizens on editorial boards and organize focus groups to glean their ideas on what should be covered.

Several independent organizations have set up review procedures of their own. Accuracy in Media (AIM) and the Media Research Center hunt for liberal tilt in the media. Fairness & Accuracy in Reporting (FAIR) looks for creeping corporate and conservative control over the news. According to the *American Journalism Review,* the left-leaning Institute for Media Analysis has a self-proclaimed mission of battling misleading reporting, particularly in the New York *Times.* Other watchdogs have included the National Organization for Women's Media Project and Lesbian and Gay Media Advocates, which monitor coverage of women and gays, respectively.

These groups shed light on journalistic shortcomings. But they do not do much to encourage journalists to invite outside criticism such as news councils. Instead they raise the old concern that guardians of the guardians, if given half a chance, will pursue their own biases and thereby tether the public's watchdog.

## Why Libel Terrifies the Press

Libel, technically speaking, results from publication of a falsehood injurious to someone's reputation. Journalists would just as soon define it as a fast way to spend lots of money, damage their own reputations, and put a damper on courageous reporting.

The Constitution as well as the superstructure of laws built on it are not designed to curtail aggressive reporting. Journalists have the right to report wrongdoing and even to ridicule, especially if the subject is a public official. To ensure journalists can be aggressive in pursuing stories, the law even allows them to be inaccurate.

Still, not everything goes, and the legal ground is constantly shifting around libel. What's more, journalists are acutely aware that they face the threat of costly and time-consuming lawsuits even if they have exercised great caution in what they write.*

Start with the shifting legal protections for comment on public officials. Truth has long been a defense against charges that a journalist has committed libel. But what if a journalist mistakenly reports defamatory information that is not true? Until 1964 journalists worked under libel laws that varied from state to state. That year, in a historic case (*New York Times Co.* v. *Sullivan*), the U.S. Supreme Court ruled that the Constitution covered libel. Under the ruling, public officials could not recover damages for defamation concerning their conduct unless the journalist knowingly made false statements or unless false statements were made with reckless disregard for the truth. Such malicious recklessness is difficult to prove because it is difficult to know what is in a reporter's mind when writing the story. The Supreme Court saw fit to give the benefit of doubt to journalists in the interests of ensuring energetic debate on political issues, a keen interest of the nation's Founders.

The constitutional protection in the 1964 ruling has evolved in ways that help and hinder journalists. Three years later the Supreme Court broadened the defense against libel by including comment not only on public officials but also on public *figures,* that is, not only elected and appointed officials but celebrities and others who make their living in the public eye. Subsequently, though, the Court has narrowed definitions of public figures. In one libel case, lower courts ruled that a scientist who sought and received public funds for

---

* "The average libel judgment increased from less than $500,000 in 1987–88 to $4 million in 1989–90 and $8 million in 1990–91 and decreased to $1 million in 1992-93," according to the Newspaper Association of America's 1994 *Facts About Newspapers.*

research should be treated as a public figure. The Supreme Court disagreed.

<u>Private individuals have more protection than public ones</u>. As discussed in the next chapter, their personal lives are just that, personal. When a hardware store owner speaks out at a town meeting on garbage collection, he becomes a public figure only in that setting. In suing for defamation on matters relating to his private life, he need only prove carelessness on the part of a reporter, not malice, to collect damages.

Journalists under some circumstances may repeat libelous statements made by others. <u>They may quote defamatory statements made in courts or at official meetings, such as national and state legislative sessions. In those settings the speakers have "absolute privilege," meaning they can't be sued for defamation</u>; <u>journalists, in turn, have "conditional privilege," meaning they can quote the libelous statements so long as those quotes are accurate and the overall reporting is full and fair.</u> Should a legislator say something defamatory about a private citizen at a Rotary Club luncheon, not on the floor of the House of Representatives, the situation is not the same. The legislator is in potential trouble and so is the newspaper if it prints the libel. If the plaintiff is a public person, then he or she must still prove actual malice in order to prevail in court.

Privileged information is the basis for reporting crime news. Even here, though, journalists must be careful not to fall into libel. People are arrested for *allegedly* stealing, and journalists must be careful to identify the suspects correctly. If someone is brought in for questioning by the police and not charged, that must be clearly indicated. The courts determine guilt or innocence. Journalists, of course, report verdicts.

Along with the First Amendment ferment over libel have come ever bigger and more aggressive lawsuits. In some cases judgments have run into the millions of dollars, although these judgments are usually reversed or sharply reduced on appeal. (One study, for instance, has shown that only 7 percent of those public figures who bring libel suits actually win.) But the costs to newspapers are great even when they prevail. <u>The average price tag of defending a libel case today is about $150,000</u>. Little wonder the escalating costs of libel insurance are outstretching the budgets of smaller newspapers. Even when a newspaper has an entirely verifiable story, journalists complain, editors may be reluctant to publish it for fear of a costly libel suit. This has had what the press calls a "chilling effect" on investigative journalism conducted for the public good.

Legal scholars have recently suggested new remedies to deal with libel. These have included printing more corrections in the newspaper, limiting financial damages, and requiring the losing side to pay all legal costs. "American libel law manages to achieve the worst of two worlds," libel scholar Floyd Abrams has commented. "It does little to protect reputation. It does much to deter speech."

## Why the Line Between Public and Private Is a Tightrope

We've talked about how pushy journalists must be to do their jobs. We've not talked about the soul-searching involved in invading people's privacy. Here is columnist Anna Quindlen agonizing over the media's revelation that tennis star Arthur Ashe had AIDS: "I feel like one of those cartoon characters who has a little angel on one shoulder and little devil on the other. The reporter—the one some people would say is carrying the pitchfork—says one thing, the human being another."

Every day the drive to publish news runs smack into people's "right to be let alone," as Supreme Court justice Louis D. Brandeis and S. D. Warren described the right to privacy in an 1890 article in the *Harvard Law Review*. The problem isn't made any easier by the lack of traffic signals.

The Supreme Court has published clear, if still evolving, opinions on such issues as libel. It has not been nearly so definitive on privacy. The idea of privacy as a legal concept did not begin until the Brandeis-Warren article, and it subsequently took hold slowly. Today privacy laws involving the press cover such issues as intrusion into one's solitude (reporters entering your house uninvited or using a telephoto lens to photograph you lounging unsuspectingly by your fenced-in pool), publicizing embarrassing private facts that would be highly offensive to a reasonable person and not of legitimate concern to the public (reporters revealing details of your income tax to illustrate the impact of new tax policies on the average citizen), or placing someone in a false light (a photo of looting during a riot that shows a woman carrying a television set she actually paid for). But the laws vary widely from state to state, and even then aggrieved citizens often find it difficult to win privacy cases.

Meanwhile, there is wide scope within the law for journalists to exercise their own judgment. "We're not going over the line here—and where's the line anyway?" said Kansas City *Star* editor Arthur S. Brisbane of reporting on Ashe's illness. "It keeps moving."

Readers believe the line has moved too far. Seventy-seven percent of those interviewed in a 1989 Times Mirror poll said the press invades people's privacy. Nevertheless, the little devil perched on journalists' shoulders is having its day. Journalists said nothing about President Franklin Roosevelt's extramarital affairs and, out of deference to his office, were careful not to photograph the polio-crippled chief of state in such a way that his wheelchair was visible. Now, spurred on by President Lyndon Johnson lifting his shirt to display the scar from his gallbladder operation, journalists demand full details on every presidential health checkup. President Reagan's operation for colon cancer prompted vivid graphics in the newspapers across the country. Meanwhile, any presidential aspirant knows that sexual dalliances can bring out squads of reporters looking for details. And juvenile suspects are more frequently identified in the press, as Alicia C. Shepard noted in the *American Journalism Review:* "In years past, it would have been unthinkable to identify a child charged with any crime, serious or not. Minors, it was argued, had a better chance of rehabilitation if they weren't stigmatized. But today, as more juveniles kill, rape and rob, news managers seem to have a much less difficult time naming them."

The law on privacy makes an important distinction between public officials and private citizens. Because the former voluntarily make their living in the public eye, their lives are especially newsworthy. They have *almost* no protection. Hounded by Ron Galella, an aggressive photographer of the rich and famous, Jacqueline Kennedy Onassis went to court. Galella was ordered to stay twenty-five feet from her and thirty feet from her children. But in a case such as that involving Ashe in 1992, journalists must answer only to the court of their own conscience. The verdict varies.

Ashe knew for four years that he had been infected by a blood transfusion—and so did a number of journalists, including *Newsweek* sports reporter Frank Deford and *Today* host Bryant Gumbel. Then someone tipped off the *USA Today* tennis reporter—a childhood friend of Ashe's—about the illness. The reporter called Ashe for confirmation. Ashe demurred at first, but, realizing the story was now likely to come out anyway, he decided to call a press conference. "I didn't commit any crimes, and I'm not running for public office," he complained to the press. "I should be able to reserve the right to keep things like that [illness] private."

In response, journalists who reported the story asked what would have been appropriate if Ashe had been hospitalized in a car accident or operated on for cancer. He is one of the most famous athletes of the century; the press would have had to cover those stories. So why not his illness?

Those who have not sought the public eye may have a better chance of protecting their privacy, but they are hardly immune from finding themselves in the news. Not only do newspapers have an absolute right to publish embarrassing private facts found in public records but they also work under a broader umbrella that says they can report other *newsworthy* information about a private person.

As a general rule, media scholar Louis Day has noted, "anything that takes place in public view can be reported. The idea is that activities that transpire in public are, by definition, not private." This means that a newspaper photographer looking for a good shot to illustrate the first day of spring may well take a picture of a couple kissing on a park bench. A sensitive journalist will check to see whether they are married to each other, not to other people.* But a photographer has no legal requirement to do so.

When reporters first started to interview newsworthy people for stories in the middle of the nineteenth century, critics howled that this "contrivance" was an invasion of privacy. Today interviews seem quite tepid in comparison to the decisions editors must make. Consider the case of a blazing house and the photo showing the anguish of a horror-stricken mother who has just learned her children could not be saved. Fires are newsworthy, but should the paper show the private grief of the mother? Or how about the photo of a woman who runs nearly naked from a house where she has been held captive? A Florida appellate court said she could not recover damages, but some journalists wonder whether that photo went too far.

---

\* If the photograph gives a false impression that the two are married to each other, the photographer might still be sued for "false light" invasion of privacy.

Rape is an especially controversial area. The crime is an extreme violation of a woman's privacy; a news story about rape can be embarrassing because of the social stigma attached to it. The law does not offer much help in deciding what a newspaper should do. Only six states have laws that prohibit publication of rape victims' names, and in any event the Supreme Court has ruled that if a name is released by public officials or is in the public record, it can be published in the newspaper. As a result, <u>publishing the names of rape victims is an ethical more than a legal problem for newspapers.</u> Most will not publish rape victims' names without their consent, but many also worry about the implications of that policy. Rape is a crime, crime is news, and news is what journalists are supposed to report. Also, by withholding names of rape victims, newspapers help perpetuate the stigma, says Geneva Overholser, former editor of the Des Moines *Register.* She argues that newspapers should publish names and graphic details about rapes so as to demolish those taboos.

"As rough and unruly and uncomfortable as it is, this is what we're supposed to be doing," Overholser observed. "If you think about the things that are the most difficult for people—rape victims' names or Arthur Ashe's AIDS—this is how society makes change. Our role is not to suppress difficult information. We've got to be willing to offend people. We should be in the business of telling people what we know."

But this is not the last word. Overholser may argue that a rape victim's name should be published, but under her stewardship the Des Moines *Register* only did so if the victim consented.*

---

* Journalists' discomfort in dealing with privacy is no less acute when their own lives become news. In 1995 Overholser resigned as editor of the *Register,* citing the bottom-line loss considerations that have become so prevalent in newsrooms. In the slew of national stories that followed, the Gannett-owned paper looked bad; Overholser looked good. In the words of the *Wall Street Journal,* she became "something of a journalism folk hero." Then it was learned that her resignation may have involved another factor as well: she and the managing editor, who had resigned at the same time, were divorcing their spouses and, an investigation of real estate records showed, buying a house together in Washington, D.C. To a *Register* reporter who looked into the story, she responded, "Why my personal life as a private citizen in Washington, D.C., interests you or your readers is absolutely beyond me." However unfair she thought the news stories (she argued the decision to divorce came weeks after the resignations), Overholser retracted the re-

# Why They Didn't Publish Your Letter to the Editor

You're hopping mad about something you read in the newspaper. Maybe it wasn't a mistake by the paper but a really stupid remark by a politician reported in the news pages. In any case, you don't want the remark to go by without strong comment. What can you do about it?

In the United States, the acceptable recourse is not burning down the building. You write "a letter to the editor" of the offending newspaper with the hope that it will be published. You carefully craft the letter, making your points clearly and concisely, sign your name, and list your address at the bottom, as the instructions in the newspaper typically say.* Then you mail it and wait. And wait. Days go by without the letter being published. You finally get up the gumption to call the newspaper to find out why.

At a big-city paper, it is not actually the editor who receives those letters but a fairly low-level employee of the editorial department responsible for the opinion and commentary pages. The top editor—the one in charge of the newsroom, which may even be on a different floor than the editorial department—might eventually see the letter, but not before it and scores of other letters have been vetted elsewhere.

Thus, when you make your call, it is probably directed to that underling in the editorial department, who promises to relay your complaint to the "person in charge." At a large paper, that might be an editorial page editor; at a small-town paper, you may reach the overall editor. Either way, here is what you are likely to be told when one of these people gets back to you:

• "We are under no obligation to print your letter. We decide what goes in the paper." This is true. There is no "right of reply" in the American press. But most newspapers would give a reason because they want to maintain good relations with their reading public. One of the

---

mark that her private affairs were not anyone's business. As she had said long before, "Newspapers aren't worth a damn if they don't invade people's privacy."

＊ Studies of newspaper use of letters to the editor show certain rules to be widespread. Virtually all papers insist on the writers signing the letters; most prefer that letters do not run more than two hundred to three hundred words and will edit them for length. Most will correct grammatical and spelling errors. Eighty-five percent don't publish poetry.

chief reasons they run letters is to develop their ties with readers. This is why many newspapers limit the number of letters they will publish from any single reader.

• "I'm sorry, but we've had a number of letters about the same subject. We can't print them all." Space might not permit it, and no one wants to read a lot of letters that say pretty much the same thing. In such instances, the editor will take a representative sample of reader opinion, often trying to get balance on various sides of an issue just as in news stories, and discard the rest.

• "That's a good letter but not particularly relevant to readers." Studies show that editors are partial to letters that relate to the community. As a resident of Buffalo Springs, Idaho, you have as much right as anyone to comment on the secretary general of the United Nations. And if the letter is clever or brimming with insight, it may end up in the paper. But comments on the mayor and how the city council is wasting your tax dollars have a better chance of being printed. Similarly, about one-third of the newspapers polled in one study said they wouldn't run letters by readers who live outside the paper's circulation area.

• "Your letter missed the point: You criticized us for quoting something a politician said. We may not agree with him, but he said it. That is what is called news." The newspaper does have a point. People often make the mistake of blaming the messenger for the message.

• "We can't publish that. It's libelous!" Perhaps you got a little carried away in calling your neighbors "certifiable nut-cases." Newspapers are cautious about saying things that can get them hauled into court for libel.* Of course, if they really like your letter, they can and often do edit out offensive sections.

• "We didn't feel like publishing it, and it's none of your damned business why!" This is an unlikely reply in today's customer-service climate, but if you do get one like it, it might confirm your suspicion that the offending politician is indeed a golfing buddy of the publisher.

---

*The first known lawsuit involving a letter to the editor was occasioned by a congressman named Mathew Lyons, who wrote a letter to the editor in 1789, accusing President John Adams of "unbounded thirst for ridiculous pomp, foolish adulation, or selfish avarice." Lyons was hauled up on a charge of violating the Sedition Act, fined one thousand dollars, and sent to jail for four months. Such comment today would not land the writer in jail or, probably, even on a talk show.

Letters to the editors are today seen as part of the democratic ideal in which people can give voice to their opinions. But the origins of newspaper letters are quite different. In the eighteenth century and well into the nineteenth century, they were published as a form of news reporting and a way to foment revolution. Pamphleteers, often writing as John Dickinson did in his "Letters from a Farmer in Pennsylvania," stirred up trouble in newspapers during the Revolutionary War. Many writers, like Benjamin Franklin, wrote anonymously. The modern idea of letters to the editor—letters from average readers rather than political firebrands—actually did not appear until the beginning of this century. The New York *Times* didn't publish letters to the editor regularly until 1931.

Such sections are not only a standard feature of newspapers today but they have grown in popularity. Editors are publishing more letters on the editorial page, and some papers have special letters sections in more than one part of the paper—say, the books section and the sports section as well as the editorial page. These sections have good readership. The Palm Beach *Post* uses a full page of letters on Saturdays. According to one study, letters to the editor had higher readership than the sports or business pages.

Just because the public likes to read letters and eager-to-please editors are publishing more of them doesn't mean you have a better chance of getting *yours* in print. You have a lot of competition. For example, the Portland *Oregonian,* with a weekday circulation of 330,000, receives fifty to seventy-five letters a day and uses an average of nine.

So, if the answer to your letter is no, you might want to try some of the options mentioned in the following section on the news consumer's bill of rights. These, too, provide better outlets for your anger than burning down the building.

······················································

## Aside: The News Consumer's Bill of Rights

Like other consumers, newspaper readers have rights. These rights may not be written down in the Constitution and they may not be "inalienable," but they exist just the same.

You have a right to:

• write a publishable letter of complaint to the editor. If your letter is reasonable and doesn't libel anyone, it may be printed.

• write a letter directly to the publisher. As the top boss, the publisher doesn't usually investigate a complaint personally (unless he or she is your friend). It will likely be passed down the line for a response, but because it came from the publisher, you can be pretty sure it will get answered in a courteous way.

• demand a correction or retraction. If you can demonstrate that the paper erred in a matter of provable fact, most newspapers will probably print a correction. They don't like making mistakes either, and the offending writer or editor will be informed and possibly reprimanded. It is much more difficult to get a paper to retract an interpretation or an editorial opinion.

• refuse to grant an interview if requested. There is no law that says a private citizen has to talk to the press. You may have to talk in front of the press, as in a court of law, but you can always blow off an interviewer.

• refuse to be interviewed by a specific reporter. You have the right to ask who is working on a story before agreeing to cooperate. If you don't like a certain reporter's work, you can simply refuse to play. Editors and reporters don't like their judgment questioned, but it's within your power to do it. If you have doubts about a journalist, you can hire one of the firms that have sprung up to report on reporters and their biases.*

• tape the taper. Pull out your own recorder.

• ask to see the story before it's published. Journalists really hate this, but if they want you to talk badly enough, they should be willing to bargain. Many newspapers have house rules against showing sources stories before publication, but you can at least demand that your quotes be read to you on the phone before the story goes to press.

• order a reporter out of your house and off your property. Trespassing is still illegal in the United States.

• cancel your subscription. Publishers and business managers hate this one, because it hurts them where it counts—in the pocket-

---

* Unless, of course, you are a government official. Hazel O'Leary, Department of Energy secretary during the Clinton administration, hired a firm called Carma to dope out journalists who covered her. The cost to taxpayers was $46,500. When the *Wall Street Journal* broke the story in late 1995, reporters had a field day. O'Leary had to reimburse the government out of her own pocket.

book. Threaten to get your friends to cancel their subscriptions, too. Don't do this too often, though. They may not renew it once you cool down.

• picket the newspaper office. But get a police permit first, and don't trespass or disturb the peace.

• take legal action. Suing for libel is most typical. Just the threat might bring reconsideration if it appears you can make a good case. One Nevada judge had a more creative legal way to deal with a paper that had been criticizing him in editorials. When the *Daily Sparks Tribune* delivered free papers as part of a promotion, the judge formally determined that the unsolicited newspaper was "garbage" and therefore had been unlawfully left on driveways under city law. He fined the paper $1,000.

## Why Your Complaint Is Taken Seriously

News consumers often say their complaints fall on deaf ears when they write or phone the editor about an offensive story. The truth is, gripes from the public are often taken very seriously.

One of the authors, as a cub reporter, once described a frequent critic of local government as a "gadfly." (This was the type of person—every town should have one—who showed up at almost every public meeting to pick apart a policy or regulation.) The critic looked up the definition of *gadfly* in his dictionary and wrote the editor the following: "A gadfly is a fly that bites cattle. I am not a gadfly." The editor ran an apology in the next edition.

Publishers have become increasingly sensitive to reader complaints. Better to deal informally with a reader who feels abused by the news than to sort out a costly libel case in the courts. And even if libel is not threatened, some articles and commentary draw such strong public reaction that the newspaper takes extraordinary pains to set things straight. The Washington *Post* ran the following correction February 2, 1993: "An article yesterday characterized followers of television evangelists as largely poor, uneducated and easy to command. There is no factual basis for that statement." In addition, *Post* ombudsman Joann Byrd wrote a long article explaining the genesis of the single offending sentence in the newspaper's long article about evangelical Christians. She attributed the problem to stereotypical thinking that went unnoticed at several levels of editing.

Increasingly, readers with computers and modems can reach editors and reporters directly by E-mail. A hot but reasoned message coming directly to the journalist's computer is hard to dodge. No excuses here that the telephone slip was lost or that spilled coffee obliterated the return address on the letter. Also no envelopes to lick, which means it is easy to bang out a quick response. Some newspapers, in fact, encourage reporters to respond via E-mail to readers' criticism and queries. And reporters find this a good way to turn up new angles on a story. In mid–1995 disgruntled readers of some ninety newspapers could fire off an angry note to editors via the Internet.

This doesn't mean readers will always know what action was taken. Without any announcement or correction or letter to the editor, a reporter or editor may be quietly fired for violating internal regulations or ethics in the handling of the news. It has happened scores of times in recent years, according to journalism review magazines that appoint themselves guardians of the profession.

Surprising as it may seem, a paper is more dependent upon the public for keeping it honest than the critics realize. A good example of this was the editor who received in his office a delegation of angry local realtors, complaining that the newspaper was "antidevelopment." The editor said that was nonsense, but after looking at a sampling of back issues, he came to the same conclusion. There was a pattern of negativity in almost every story written about local development. He just hadn't seen it. He ordered a review of real estate coverage, reminding his staff of the paper's policy of objectivity. The result was a noticeable reduction in negative coverage.

One reason the public is such a valuable ally in maintaining journalistic integrity is that editors cannot easily check the veracity of their reporters' information. The pressure of daily deadlines makes it particularly difficult. If a reporter writes that someone said something, an editor usually has to accept it on face value—unless the public says something different.

It would behoove the reader to keep in mind a general principle professed in the news marketplace today: "It is YOUR newspaper." So readers should feel free to complain.

# VIII

..............................

# Trends

# Why Sports Stories Wait to Tell You the Score

Try as they might, newspapers simply can't ignore television. There was a time when they dismissed the "idiot box" as a poor substitute for the written word. But today newspapers not only accept the influence of television in American life, in many instances they depend upon it.

Newspapers have taken their cue from television to give themselves a face-lift. They've added color, shortened stories, put greater emphasis on graphics, and changed the definition of news. Vending machines for *USA Today* look like television sets.

Perhaps television's most profound influence on the print media has been to diminish the element of time. A popular ground rule of the newspaper industry used to be "get it right, but get it first." Today it is a rare occasion when a paper gets a major breaking story to the public before the electronic media do. With television now allowed inside courtrooms and legislatures (including Congress), with the growth of community coverage on cable, and with the introduction of the Minicam, there are few places television reporters cannot go.

In the old days, sports reporters told readers the score of the game in the first paragraph. Today sports writers assume that most fans have already seen the big game on the tube and know who won. The writer for tomorrow's edition can ease into the story without pummeling the audience with facts it already knows. This same trend appears with breaking news. Reporters look deeper to find new angles in stories broken by television. Nowadays, you can find social-trend stories on page one that are not tied to specific events.

Seeing television as competitors for consumers' attention, newspapers initially were reluctant to run daily television programming schedules. Today they realize some people buy the newspaper so they can find out what to watch on TV. Newspapers employ television critics and run news stories on television programs and stars and even syndicated synopses of the soaps. And as much as it may hurt their egos, newspaper journalists do get news from the TV set. Sometimes they use television for tips on what needs to be covered. Sometimes television makes the news. When Ross Perot announced on CNN's *Larry King Live* that he would consider running for president, it became front-page news across the country. This became a pattern during the campaign. Observed the *National Journal,* "Print reporters are confined to writing about what Perot does on TV."

Television does command a large audience. In the average American household, according to one commonly cited statistic, the television is on more than seven hours a day. The average prime-time American TV program routinely reaches more than 15 million viewers. While those television sets are not always turned to the news, TV news rivals newspapers. That Larry King program with Perot had 3.5 million viewers. In 1994, according to the Freedom Forum Media Studies Center, "72 percent of Americans said they got most of their news from television, compared to just 38 percent who said newspapers. Some 45 percent said that television was their only source of news."

The advent of television has ushered in fears of the printed word becoming obsolete the way moveable type put monks out of the business of illuminating manuscripts. The United States ranks lowest of all the industrialized states in reading ability. "Anyone connected to the publishing industry worries about the future," says Richmond *Times-Dispatch* book editor Ann Merriman. "An appalling illiteracy rate and the younger generation's preference for the visual images of television offer little cause for optimism that the written word will prevail for long as a major means of communication."

Newspapers have found plenty of data to set them worrying about their written products prevailing. Between 1970 and 1994, weekday newspaper readers declined from 77 percent of the population to 61 percent, according to the Newspaper Association of America. The amount of time spent reading the paper has also declined. One recent study says the average is 35 minutes a day, compared to 53 minutes in the 1940s. Others are far less generous in their estimates, saying the average reader is spending no more than 20 minutes.

The realization that people were spending less time with the newspaper helped inspire Gannett's design of *USA Today* in 1982. Since then, other newspapers also have worked harder to become more "visual." As noted earlier, <u>reporters are expected to come back to the newsroom with the facts for a story *and* with ideas for a chart or graph to illustrate the report.</u> Newspapers have purchased expensive color printing presses and hired more graphic artists. Even the New York *Times,* one of the few papers without comics and political cartoons, has invested $400 million in a color production facility to spruce up its "gray lady" image.

In some respects, newspapers will never best television. The TV will always be more colorful. And it has an advantage in showing action scenes. How many writers can capture the excitement of a 95-yard broken-field run for a touchdown seen on television or the drama of O. J. Simpson's white Ford Bronco racing down the freeway?

But newspapers are far from obsolete. Statistics on readership can be read in ways that are positive. Here is what James Shelledy says about the Salt Lake *Tribune,* which he edits. Considering that the paper has 2.5 readers for every copy circulated, Shelledy says, "I have a morning audience equal to the [local] audiences of all four evening newscasts combined." Others note similar national trends. "There are more people who read newspapers every day than watch early evening network newscasts, early evening local newscasts, or late evening local newscasts," report Thomas Hargrove of Scripps Howard and Guido H. Stempel of Ohio University. And the numbers for newspapers may be improving. For one thing, Shelledy says, studies show that baby boomers are reading more and watching television less.

Newspapers can do many things better than television.* They are better suited to hard news reporting, investigative journalism, and news analysis. They have more room to be comprehensive, to present the details and context of a story. The national/international

---

\* Communications specialist Neil Postman has made a strong case that television ruins public discourse. "On one hand, there is the world of the printed word with its emphasis on logic, sequence, history, exposition, objectivity, detachment, and discipline. On the other, there is the world of television with its emphasis on imagery, narrative, presentness, simultaneity, intimacy, immediate gratification, and quick emotional response."

newsholes of the Atlanta *Constitution* and the Des Moines *Register* are twice as large as the newsholes of the networks' evening news. The high cost of television production, as well as space and time limitations, tends to discourage a commitment to extensive analysis and investigation. In addition, words are more conducive to reasoned argument and analysis than are visual images. In fact, highly charged visual images sometimes interfere.

Newspapers provide services that network television does not: birth, wedding, and obituary announcements, classified ads, government notices, box scores for sporting events, comprehensive stock market quotes, comics, horoscopes, movie times, and TV show listings.

Television finds it much more difficult to provide meaningful commentary. Networks are reluctant to take controversial editorial positions for fear of offending viewers (readers can skip over editorial pages they don't like; television editorials stare viewers right in the face, like it or not). At the local level, when a station takes an editorial stand, it is expected to invite opposing views. Not paying attention to such matters can be costly. Since broadcasters are required to obtain government licenses in order to operate, and because their impact is so wide-reaching, their policies and practices have come under particular scrutiny by Congress and the Federal Communications Commission, which regulates them. When it comes to influence over powerbrokers, Shelledy says, "the newspaper has it all over television."

This comparative strength of newspapers should not be surprising. The missions of newspapers and television are quite different. "Unlike every newspaper in America, the fundamental business of a television network is not news," wrote Grant Tinker and Bud Rukeyser, former NBC executives. "Television networks, whose only income is from advertisers who want to reach the largest possible number of viewers, are in the mass-appeal business."

Not that newspapers feel secure. Nearly fifty years after the television age began, the print press is still uncertain about its place and future in the American mass media. A lobbyist for the Newspaper Association of America was recently overheard identifying himself to a congressman: "Hi, I represent the dinosaurs." Meanwhile, newspaper executives are working hard to find new news formulas that will attract readers.

# Why Michael Jackson's New Hairdo Is Front-Page News

When this country was young, news was serious stuff. The long, gray news columns were read by sober-minded and respectable businessmen. Newspapers were devoid of anything mildly entertaining.

That began to change about the middle of the last century when the daily paper became a mass medium, offering something for everybody in a mass-educated, mass-marketed society. The concept of entertaining one's readers while informing them was part of the formula for success spawned by the popular "penny press" in an increasingly urbanized America. The new game was to attract as many readers as possible.

Joseph Pulitzer, one of the foremost newspaper innovators of the nineteenth century, bought the solid but uncompetitive New York *World* in the 1880s and employed reporters who looked for "human-interest" news, the more sensational the better. "There is room in this great and growing city for a journal that is not only cheap but bright," explained Pulitzer in announcing his purchase of the paper. When the newspaper's circulation reached 100,000, he had a hundred-gun salute fired in Central Park and gave a tall silk hat to each of his employees. By the turn of the century, newspapers were beginning to provide separate sports sections, regular titled humor columns, and large Sunday newspapers with color comics.*

This transformation did not mean that the "funnies" drove out hard news. On the contrary, trendsetters like Pulitzer saw the need for a healthy mix of copy. While the *World* was sponsoring "stunt" reporter Nellie Bly's trip around the world, serious news remained the "backbone of the paper," in the words of historian Frank Luther Mott. The famous 1920s editor Herbert Bayard Swope described his task as holding a middle ground between two forces: "What I try to do in my paper is to give the public part of what it wants to have and part of what it ought to have, whether it wants it or not."

The proper balance between fact and fun has remained a dominant worry in the news business. In the 1940s, Oswald Garrison Villard

---

* The first six-days-a-week comic strip was H. C. Fisher's, which came to be known as "Mutt and Jeff." It debuted in the San Francisco *Chronicle* on November 15, 1907.

decried the consequences of commercialization of the news product and "the continuing change [of newspapers] from a purely informative and news-printing medium into an organ of entertainment as well." The famous Hutchins commission, set up about the same time to evaluate media, came to the same conclusion. "The American newspaper is now as much a medium of entertainment, specialized information, and advertising as it is of news. . . . Hence the word 'news' has come to mean something different from important new information."

As anyone looking at newspaper trade organs such as *Editor & Publisher* notices, this debate has heated up in recent years. In a 1994 article in *E&P,* James P. Gannon, recently retired Washington bureau chief of the Detroit *News,* argued that the press has gone too far in one direction. Newspapers, he wrote, "are increasingly substituting entertainment values for news values. . . . Our business is news, not entertainment." A contrary view in those same pages came from Al Neuharth. There was no golden age of journalism, he wrote. Entertainment has always been a news value. Newspapers, he concluded, "are better than ever. The theory that newspaper standards are declining is both ahistorical and wrong."

Those who agree with Gannon tick off a long list of sins, which are commonly lumped together under the rubric "infotainment." A newspaper, they argue, could just as well feature a celebrity profile on the front page, along with a fetching photo, a sports highlight, a dieting hint, a report on the latest mall opening, and a cartoon graphic on how you spend your money, all in living color. Old-timers know that the weather is news, but they inveigh against the "color weather map," which is a symbol of selling out news values for visuals. Across the country diehards quarrel with publishers who want to put the arrival of the Wonderbra at the local mall on the front page. Herbert Bayard Swope, these diehards say, would swoon.

No doubt about it, what-happened-yesterday is no longer the undisputed criterion for front-page news. Now editors consider not only trend stories but also whether a story is intrinsically interesting and provocatively presented to their audience. In the past, newspaper editors knew what the people wanted and needed, or at least they thought they did. Today they use focus groups and other marketing techniques to find out what interests readers. As a result, Michael Jackson's new hairdo becomes front-page news.

Many editors defend themselves by saying that they still do provide important news, even when it is dull. Still others think that changes in newspapers are exciting. "In place of the Old News, something dramatic is evolving, a new culture of information, a hybrid New News— dazzling, adolescent, irresponsible, fearless, frightening and powerful," media critic Jon Katz wrote approvingly for *Rolling Stone* magazine. In his opinion, the journalist is no longer in the front seat of history. "Bart Simpson's critique of society is more trenchant than that of most newspaper columnists," Katz wrote.

Anne Wells Branscomb, a research associate at Harvard Law School's Program on Information Resources Policy, notes the value of entertainment as an effective means of education. "Infotainment," she says, "is really the right direction to go, in terms of raising the level of comprehension of the population."

The controversy will not end soon. But more and more often it will be carried out of the newsrooms and onto the golf courses. Those early-retirement packages that newspapers offer during restructuring can look attractive to the old pros who don't like change in the newsroom.

# Why Champagne Prices Are News

How can a business go "downmarket" at the same time it is going "upscale"? The newspaper industry knows. The new formula for economic survival in the print media is to attract the upscale spending public by appealing to its downmarket interests.

Marketing is the gospel. The conventional wisdom in newspaper marketing circles is that the big-spending post-boomer generation between the ages of eighteen and thirty-five is less interested in weighty matters of state and other traditional staples of news than in quality-of-life issues. If newspapers are going to hold and gain the readers that advertisers want to reach, news reporting must be more consumer oriented. This new philosophy means that a newspaper may run a special section with a story on champagne drinking trends, hold a reader lottery for a case of the finest bubbly, and publish a four-color ad from the local wine store.

*Packaging* has become a dominant word in the newspaper industry. It refers to the wrapping or design of the paper. The design specialists, now using a computer to "lay out" the paper more creatively, are sometimes paid more than editors today. It also means the newspaper is presenting information more thematically, sectioning certain types of news for certain types of people. For example, Spanish-speaking readers can find *La Raza Domingo* in the Chicago *Sun-Times, Nuestro Tiempo* in the Los Angeles *Times,* or *El Nuevo Tiempo* in the Santa Barbara *News-Press.* The Fort Lauderdale *Sun-Sentinel*'s magazine *Tilt,* for people in their late twenties, debuted in 1995.

This is a change from the past when newspapers looked at their audience as a somewhat anonymous, monolithic group with general interests and needs. While newspapers are not abandoning news suitable for a mass audience, they are thinking more like big consumer-minded corporations and hiring people who have that orientation. Mark Willes is an example. In 1995, the former General Mills vice-chairman became chief executive officer of the Times Mirror Company, which owns the Los Angeles *Times,* the Baltimore *Sun,* and *Newsday.* Shortly after his appointment, Willes said newspapers needed to think more about meeting readers' needs in the way that manufacturers of breakfast food and cake mixes do.

"You want to know as much about them [readers] as possible, and then tailor the message accordingly," says Carol Ann Riordan, associate director at the American Press Institute. "Let's say you want to target your message to professional women who work outside the home, have two children, live in the suburbs, and enjoy a combined income of $100,000. Put together the paper with that person in mind, and you'll get the readers and advertisers you want. But you've got to push the hot buttons."

This technique is called "relationship" marketing, because it relies on building long-term relationships with certain types of readers instead of sending a scatter-shot message to everyone. To identify the preferred customer and start building a relationship, newspapers are using databases to collect as much demographic and financial information about their customers as possible. They are buying credit card lists, sending out detailed questionnaires, and conducting phone surveys. This targeting can also attract more advertisers. After examining advertisers' needs, for instance, Milwaukee's *Journal Sentinel* created eight neighborhood sections.

The impact of this new marketing religion is being felt in the newsroom as well. More consumer advice, shoppers' guides, and money-management counseling are appearing on the news pages. One paper in California, the Orange County *Register,* started a "mall beat" where the reporter roamed shopping centers in search of news.

The old newsroom walls between "church" (news) and "state" (business) are being dismantled in an effort to integrate the once-conflicting interests of the industry. "The myth of the editor being corrupted by talking to an ad director is breaking down," says Jeff Cowart of the American Press Institute. More and more editors are "knee-deep in business discussions, but have not put their ethics in their backpockets."

Thomas Winship, former editor of the Boston *Globe* who writes a column in *Editor & Publisher,* calls this consumer-happy trend "the Great Downgrade." He believes, however, that consumer-driven journalism will not utterly take over the newsroom. The number of serious papers, he says, "will be smaller, but their long-range future will be secure, and their corporate soul will be intact." While the debate is far from decided, some of the evidence suggests Winship is correct.

The Boca Raton *News* recently ran a story with this headline: "Champagne Prices Soon to Explode." Said the editor, "We're the only paper in America to do an eight-inch story on that. For baby boomers who go to a lot of champagne parties, that's more interesting than whatever Jack Kemp has to say today." The story, he explained, was part of the paper's new overall approach to covering news. "Newspapers have failed to treat readers as customers and tailor the product to the interests and expectations of those customers. We have to do what Chevrolet and Ivory soap do."

His enthusiasm, however, proved excessive. The paper's experiment with such news was abandoned as a bad idea. In addition, that mall beat is no longer around. But even as some of these notions fail, other experiments in packaging come along. And some have a bright side for the future. The Detroit *Free Press*'s YAK page features articles, quizzes, and games for primary school kids. This may not be news by the standards of newspaper veterans. But after two years, the paper claimed it was winning over the young generation in the city.

••••••••••••••••••••••••••••••••••••••••••••••••••••••••••••

**Aside: Literacy**

More than thirty million American adults were believed to be illiterate in 1994, and an estimated 2.2 million are added to the rolls each year. Since there were some 195 million American adults in 1994, that would mean 15 percent of the adult population cannot read.

Newspapers have a love-hate relationship with high illiteracy rates. When press organizations want to persuade businesses to use newspapers for their advertising, they talk about how many readers they have. "In 1994, an average of over 115 million Americans (or over 61 percent of the total adult population) read a weekday newspaper, steady readership compared to 1993," proclaimed a press release from the Newspaper Association of America. When associations want to persuade their members to pay more attention to winning more readers, they put a bleak face on the statistics. The trade publication *Editor & Publisher* has said that "one in three American adults not only cannot read your newspaper or mine, he or she cannot read a job application."

Self-interest aside, literacy is difficult to track. Definitions have changed over the years. Until 1850 you were considered literate if you were able to write your own name. From then until 1900, you were literate if you could write your name and recite biblical passages from memory. From then until 1980, the ability to understand unfamiliar material was the general test. Now there is what is called an "application" standard that measures literacy according to the ability to read and write at a level required to function in society. The current working definition of an illiterate person—the one used to arrive at the 15 percent illiteracy rate mentioned above—is one who cannot read English at all or can read only the simplest signs, labels, or instructions and who cannot read beyond a third- or fourth-grade level.

Whatever newspapers say to advertisers, they are concerned about getting readers. The industry has launched an energetic campaign to improve literacy using newspapers. More than seven hundred North American newspapers sponsor Newspapers in Education programs that provide newspapers to schools at reduced rates.

••••••••••••••••••••••••••••••••••••••••••••••••••••••••••••

# Why This Isn't the End

In 1994 the Boston *Globe* decided to end the practice of having boys and girls deliver newspapers. It planned to replace the 4,300 young carriers with 2,400 adults within four years.

With so many changes, it sometimes seems the traditional newspaper itself will be replaced. Newspaper companies and professional journalism organizations are frantically exploring ways to do things differently.

The spring 1993 issue of Knight-Ridder's in-house publication, *Knight-Ridder News,* suggests the changes that are afoot. The lead article tells how Knight-Ridder's Business Information Services division provides special reports to companies "whether it's flashed onto a computer screen or splashed across the printed page." Another story is entitled "Redefining News: Knight-Ridder Newspapers Find New Ways to Connect with Readers"; it relates how one Knight-Ridder paper created a special section that appeals to women, who don't read the newspaper as much as they once did. Another article talks about the importance of stock analysts' opinions for the company's future. And the magazine profiles Roger Fidler, who at the time was running Knight-Ridder's Information Design Laboratory in Boulder, Colorado. Fidler experimented with ways to provide daily news via handheld computers. He came up with something called a newspaper tablet to replace the ink-on-paper version.

Knight-Ridder's initiatives, of course, are meant to be positive. But they are not always read that way in the newsroom. They have sent many traditional newspaper journalists heading for the door, and even those who favor change have raised some troubling questions about the future of the newspaper business. Here are four of the toughest questions.

• *Will people be less interested in the news?* In the old days Mom and Pop sat on the front porch reading the afternoon newspaper. Today both are likely to work. After buying groceries, getting the car repaired, and making a couple of runs to the day-care center, they have considerably less time to read the newspaper. (Because women bear the brunt of most of these chores, their readership in particular has declined.) Experts predict that the average American will devote 165 hours in all of 1997 to reading a newspaper, almost an 11 percent drop from 1984.

But this does not mean that Mr. and Ms. America have written off news. On the contrary, news and information on current affairs, economic and social trends, and scientific breakthroughs are all more important than ever. If people are not spending as much time at home with the newspaper, they are spending much more time at the office trying to find, absorb, and use information.

This is the Information Age. "The basic economic resource—'the means of production,' to use the economist's term—is no longer capital, nor natural resources (the economist's 'land'), nor 'labor.' *It is and will be knowledge,*" writes management guru Peter Drucker.

• *Will the newspaper survive?* People need news. But will they get that news from newspapers, or will they get it elsewhere?

One reason newspaper readership is declining is that people are so busy. Another reason is that they have so much more to read in so many different forms. "Niche" magazines and newsletters appeal to special interests. Telephone lines bring in sports scores and the latest stock quotations. "Fax" news and computer network services like Prodigy come right into home computers for a small amount of money each month.

This new technology often appears friendlier than the traditional ink-on-paper newspaper. Carriers (whether adult or kid) often fling the daily news into the bushes; newspaper ink rubs off on people's hands; and the paper itself is not particularly kind to the environment. "It took 3,100 sixty-foot trees to produce today's Atlanta *Constitution,*" notes journalism educator Ralph Lowenstein. "On any given day, old newspapers compose 7 percent to 10 percent of the municipal solid waste stream and up to 6 percent of the landfill."

All of these factors notwithstanding, the daily newspaper probably is not the dinosaur that some people make it out to be.

First, the ink-on-paper technology has pluses as well as minuses. It is easy to carry around (say, for reading on the subway or at the coffee shop), and it's easy to clip. It's also familiar. We believe the paper newspaper will survive for some time yet, even if it may be only one of several ways that the "newspaper" comes to the public.

Second, it also seems certain that the new delivery mechanisms will employ traditional newspaper concepts. The electronic newspaper on a computer screen will use some traditional layout techniques if for no other reason than subscribers will find them familiar, and traditional media companies are major actors in creating new news products. New newspapers also will rely on established formulas for determining what is news and how it is reported.

• *Will large companies dominate the news business even more than they do today?* News and information is becoming a bigger business than ever, that is certain. Who will dominate is not certain.

Traditional newspapers are becoming bigger in traditional ways. The New York *Times,* for instance, bought the also-large Boston *Globe.* Traditional newspapers are also becoming large in nontraditional ways. Consider "audiotext," which brings those sports scores over telephone lines. In 1994 about sixty newspapers offered full online versions of themselves and the number was increasing monthly. Said New York *Times* publisher Arthur Sulzberger, Jr., "I am absolutely agnostic regarding methods of distribution. . . . An electronic distribution system would not only insure that our news was an up-to-the-minute snapshot of the world's events, but it would also take hundreds of millions of dollars out of our cost structure."

Meanwhile, nontraditional media companies are getting into the news and information business. Sears, IBM, and CBS started the Prodigy Services Company. CBS was the most news-oriented of the three, but financial hard times forced it to drop out, leaving Sears and IBM as the owners. Mead Data Central, which produces a popular database called Lexis/Nexis, is a subsidiary of the Mead Corporation, a paper products company.

The possibility of large corporations dominating news is worrisome. One nightmarish question is this: If Knight-Ridder worries more and more about what the stock analysts think, will it worry less and less about high-quality news or cut back editorial staffs every time an economic crunch comes?

While the big media corporations seem to be getting bigger, however, the little fellow has more power than in the past. A printing press and circulation system is costly. But a newspaper provided via computer network to selected subscribers is not, nor is desktop publishing. Large metropolitan newspapers are finding themselves competing intensely with small operations. In the early 1990s Frank Sutherland, editor of the *Tennessean* in Nashville, estimated that some forty-seven dailies and weeklies existed in his prime readership area. They did not specialize in the big breaking stories, but they had advantages when it came to covering their segment of the community.

The emergence of light-on-their-feet smaller news operations could be a healthy development. Although the two-newspaper town is the exception rather than the rule it was in another era, competition is not dead. The new competitors can provide news that readers need. And they can keep the giants from becoming complacent and force them to be responsive to readers.

• *Will news become more fluff and less tough?* Efforts like Knight-Ridder's to "redefine the news" worry traditional journalists most of all. Special sections that appeal "to women who don't read the newspaper as much as they once did" sound suspiciously like code words for getting away from hard news. Many reporters and editors feel that journalism has lost its way when newspapers divert resources from investigative journalism in order to provide entertainment and "soft" service news (how to get the most out of your lunchtime workout) and editors play with the idea of producing scented newspapers.

The broad historical view suggests that the current debate is not as new as it sometimes sounds. Targeting news to the wishes of consumers is the reason newspapers started in the first place. As noted previously, entertainment is an old, established idea in journalism. Investigative journalism comes in waves. What is new is the intensity of the debate. New technology, changing economics and lifestyles, and other factors are *forcing* newspapers to rethink their role and approach to news.

We do not recommend nostalgia as a source of answers. In reality, that newsboy wasn't such an all-American figure.\* In the 1930s Warden Lewis Lowes testified that seven out of ten Sing Sing inmates had been newspaper boys. We do believe, though, that some of the old verities do still apply.

---

\* Mark Twain dubbed the newspaperboy "one greater than kings." In fact, many nineteenth-century carriers were waifs who slept with their heads on unsold papers, and during a 1990 strike the *Daily News* used the homeless to hawk papers on New York streets. Enterprising Thomas Edison, who sold papers on the Grand Truck Railroad, was fired (and cuffed by a conductor). Publishers have made much of giving scholarships to carriers; but when fourteen of them formed an association to bargain with the Providence *Journal-Bulletin*, management was reluctant to talk and rejected an ad the carriers wanted to pay for in the newspaper.

To our minds at least, the newspaper's unique strength is its ability to provide a wide-angled perspective on events. While specialized publications have an important role in the Information Age, people still need general news on political, business, and social issues about which they are not expert but which shape their lives. Newspapers have been far from perfect in meeting this need, but they have fulfilled the role better than anyone else. Even if "newspaper" news may come in forms other than paper, even if they improve upon their ability to entertain readers or meet their specific needs, the fundamental principles remain. We believe newspapers will not survive if they concentrate on copying television's visual glamour and brevity. Newspapers will prevail if they protect the most important part of their franchise: reliable, timely, courageous, relevant, comprehensive news about current affairs.

But the news necessary to keep economic, political, and social democracy working means nothing without active readers. For the potentials of newspapers to be realized in the future, responsibility falls on the shoulders of citizens. More than ever, readers must understand the news process—what works best and what doesn't. This knowledge might not make newspapers perform at a higher level, although we don't rule out that result. But it will lead to better-informed citizens.

# Sources

## Introduction

"He was as shy as a newspaper is when referring to its own merits." That quotation from Mark Twain's Pudd'nhead Wilson pretty well describes the self-promotional material distributed by newspapers supposedly to edify readers. The New York *Times* has its "Get More Out of Your Daily Newspaper" (by Ted M. Bernstein, 1964); the Bucks County *Courier Times* has its "How to Read a Newspaper" (no date). And most have the tone of Bernstein's "Did you ever stop to think about why you should read a newspaper?"

Over the years many books have tried to explain the inner workings of the news and the daily newspaper. Examples include Edgar Dale, *How to Read a Newspaper* (Scott, Foresman, 1941); Ivan and Carol Doig, *A News Consumer's Guide* (Prentice Hall, 1972); and Jane T. Harrigan, *Read All About It! A Day in the Life of a Metropolitan Newspaper* (Globe Pequot Press, 1987). Journalists especially have been more reverential about the news business than the facts justify, but exceptions appear, such as David Broder's Washington, D.C.-oriented *Behind the Front Page: A Candid Look at How the News Is Made* (Simon and Schuster, 1987). Some of the very best works—and more have appeared in recent years—are by people who are not members of the profession. A prime example is John Allen Paulos, *A Mathematician Reads the Newspaper* (Basic Books, 1995). One of the most thoughtful newspaper "manuals" is Robert Karl Manoff and Michael Schudson, eds., *Reading the News* (Pantheon, 1986). An entertaining general history of the news business is by journalist Loren Ghiglione, *The American Journalist: Paradox of the Press* (Library of Congress, 1990), from which this book draws anecdotal material.

For more background on specific issues cited in this introduction, readers can consult the following works. The treatment of media in college textbooks is discussed by David Stebenne, Seth Rachlin, and Martha FitzSimon in *Coverage of the Media in College Textbooks* (Freedom Forum Media Studies Center, 1992). Frederick Lewis Allen's article appeared in the *Atlantic Monthly* (January, 1922). For more discussion of the role of the press, see F. S. Siebert, T. Peterson, and W. Schramm, *Four Theories of the Press* (University of Illinois Press, 1956). The report of the Commission on Freedom of the Press is available as Robert D. Leigh, ed., *A Free and Responsible Press* (University of Chicago Press, 1947). The Lippmann quote is from *Public Opinion* (Free Press, 1922), and the Boylan quote is from "Newspeople," *Wilson Quarterly,* 1982 special issue.

# I

For a discussion of coverage of the Catholic bishop's sermon, see Charles B. Seib, Washington *Post,* February 6, 1975. The New York *Times* story on Fermat's theorem was published on June 24, 1993. An additional sign of intrepid reporting came when the reporter did a 1,500-word follow-up story on January 31, 1995. For a good discussion of distilling ideas into catch phrases like *Watergate,* see Broder's *Behind the Front Page,* Chap. 2. The "nudging, winking" quote is from Noel Annan, "Under the Victorian Bed," *New York Review of Books,* June 22, 1995. Mayer's quote is from *Making News* (Harvard Business School Press, 1993).

The Harvey Schwander story is from a little book of reminiscences about the Milwaukee *Journal* by Edwin R. Bayley, *Ask Harvey, pls* (Prairie Oak Press, 1994). The anecdote and quote "This is a god-dam lie" comes from John Hohenberg, *The News Media: A Journalist Looks at His Profession* (Holt, Rinehart and Winston, 1968); so does the quotation from Malcolm Browne on covering the Buddhist monk's suicide. Elmer Davis' quote comes from his thoughtful volume written during the Red Scare era, *But We Were Born Free* (Deutsch, 1955). The seminal book on scientific journalism is Philip Meyer's, which is now available as *The New Precision Journalism* (Indiana University Press, 1991).

The Mitchell Stephens quotation is from his book *A History of News: From the Drum to the Satellite* (Viking, 1988). Washington

*Post* editor Leonard Downie's voting habits—or lack of them—are discussed in *AP World Magazine* (Spring, 1973).

The idea of "strategic rituals" comes from Gaye Tuchman, "Objectivity as Strategic Ritual: An Examination of Newsmen's Notion of Objectivity," *American Journal of Sociology,* LXX (January, 1972).

For a good discussion of public journalism, see a pamphlet by Jay Rosen and Davis Merritt, Jr., *Public Journalism Theory and Practice* (Kettering Foundation, 1994). Also see "All Things to All People," *Editor & Publisher,* January 7, 1995. The Schram quote is found in the March 19, 1995, transcript of the CNN program "Reliable Sources." The Montgomery *Advertiser* series is described in its own story on the award it won for the effort, published April 2, 1995.

That "stunning book" on infectious diseases is by Laurie Garrett: *The Coming Plague* (Farrar, Straus and Giroux, 1994).

The concept of journalism being a "profession grafted on to an industry" comes from *A Free and Responsive Press* (Twentieth-Century Fund Task Force Report, 1973). Information on journalists' education is drawn from David Weave and G. Cleveland Wilhoit, *The American Journalist in the 1990s* (Freedom Forum, 1992). The *Nation* article "The Future of the Newspaper" appeared June 26, 1879.

## II

For historical detail on the evolution of the press in the United States, see Daniel Boorstin, *The Americans: The Colonial Experience* (Random House, 1958); Michael Emery and Edwin Emery's most recent edition of *The Press and America: An Interpretive History of the Mass Media* (Prentice Hall, 1996).

For financial data on newspapers, see *Facts About Newspapers, 95,* published by the Newspaper Association of America; *SNPA Bulletin* (January, 1993); *Editor & Publisher Yearbook,* 1994; David Pearce Demers, *Structural Pluralism, Intermedia Competition, and the Growth of the Corporate Newspaper in the United States* (Journalism Monographs, 1994).

Upton Sinclair self-published his commentary on the newspaper business in *The Brass Check: A Study of American Journalism* (Pasadena, 1919). A more recent discussion of journalism as a business is found in Doug Underwood's book *When MBAs Rule the*

*Newsroom: How Marketers and Managers Are Reshaping Today's Media* (Columbia University Press, 1993).

Quotations on the profitability of newspapers come from two sources worth consulting in their own right: Pulitzer is quoted in Tom Goldstein, *Killing the Messenger: 100 Years of Media Criticism* (Columbia University Press, 1989); and Philip Meyer in his own "Accountability When Books Make News," *Media Studies Journal* (Summer, 1992). Other sources for quotations include "More Cost-Cutting Measures for Times Mirror," *Editor & Publisher,* July 29, 1995; Richard Harwood, Washington *Post,* May 21, 1989, for the Ingersoll comment; Harwood, at the time, was ombudsman for the *Post* and wrote many columns about newspapers. The Ottaway quote is in "Chain Chairman Critical of Other Chains," *Editor & Publisher,* February 14, 1987; Winter is quoted in Jonathan Kwitney, "The High Cost of High Profits," *Washington Journalism Review* (June, 1990); the Seigenthaler quote is found in the *Congressional Record,* August 3, 1979. The Frankel quote is from Ken Auletta, *The New Yorker,* June 28, 1993. The Gannett corporate mission statement, along with Hallmark's, is from *Say It and Live It: The 50 Corporate Mission Statements That Hit the Mark* (Doubleday, 1995), by Patricia Jones and Larry Kahaner.

Details on newsprint prices come from the New York *Times,* January 16, February 2 and 18, 1995, and the *Wall Street Journal,* February 15, 1995.

The history of the *Herald Tribune* is told in Richard Kluger, *The Paper: The Life and Death of the New York Herald Tribune* (Alfred A. Knopf, 1986).

Examples of advertising pressure come from stories in the *American Journalism Review* (March and September, 1994). Additional useful background came from Leo Bogart, *Commercial Culture: The Media System and the Public Interest* (Oxford University Press, 1995); Ben H. Bagdikian, *The Media Monopoly* (Beacon Press, 1992); Philip Meyer, *Ethical Journalism: A Guide for Students, Practitioners, and Consumers* (Longman, 1987); Anthony Ramirez, New York *Times,* August 2, 1995; Angela Powers and Frederick Fico, "Influences on Use of Sources at Large U.S. Newspapers," *Newspaper Research Journal* (Fall, 1994).

"Newspaper Standards" uses data from the Scripps-Howard *General Managers Newsletter,* which has stopped its annual practice of publishing such statistics.

For a good sociological study of newspeople, see Herbert J. Gans, *Deciding What's News: A Study of CBS Evening News, NBC Nightly News, Newsweek, and Time* (Vintage, 1980).

# III

Jane Harrigan's *Read All About It!* was cited earlier; this book relates the news routines and decision-making processes that occur each day. A similar study is David Gelsanliter's *Fresh Ink: Behind the Scenes at a Major Metropolitan Newspaper* (University of North Texas Press, 1995).

A textbook discussion of layout is Russell N. Baird, Duncan McDonald, Ronald H. Pittman, and Arthur T. Turnbull's *Graphics of Communications: Methods, Media, and Technology* (Harcourt Brace Jovanovich, 1993). The story about the Pasadena *Star-News'* difficulty in ridding itself of jumps is from "The Lower Case," *Columbia Journalism Review* (March/April, 1992).

All the headlines mentioned in "Why Headlines Squeeze the Truth" are real. One of the best places to find funny heads is the back page of the monthly *Columbia Journalism Review.*

Two of Rudolf Flesch's books on writing are *The Art of Plain Talk* (Harper and Row, 1946) and *The Art of Readable Writing* (Harper and Row, 1949).

Background on *Wall Street Journal* coverage of the Fiske story can be found in the New York *Times,* April 4, 1994.

The Maugham quote is in Rene J. Cappon, *The Word* (Associated Press, 1991).

# IV

Thanks to Humphrey Taylor, chairman and CEO of Louis Harris and Associates, for the excerpt in "You Can't Count on Statistics." The Crossen quote is found in *Tainted Truth: The Manipulation of Fact in America* (Simon and Schuster, 1994). Paulos' *A Mathematician Reads the Newspaper* is a primer on how to think about the statistical aspects of the news.

The opening letter to the editor in "Why No News Is Good News" was found among old family newspaper clippings. It had no date or even the name of the newspaper in which it appeared. That someone would take the time to save the letter, which had no family news and does not appear to have been written by a family member, makes it a poignant example of public sentiment about negative news.

The Shanahan quote comes from a speech she gave in Waterville, Maine, November, 1993. The Kinsley quote appeared originally in the Washington *Post,* November 11, 1992. For a discussion of the penny press's introduction of crime news, see Andie Tucher, *Froth and Scum: Truth, Beauty, Goodness, and the Ax Murder in America's First Mass Medium* (University of North Carolina Press, 1994). The Freedom Forum First Amendment Center study was written by Beverly Kees and Bill Phillips and published by the Center in 1994 as *Nothing Sacred: Journalism, Politics, and Public Trust in a Tell-All Age.* The Times Mirror study was *The People, Their Press, and Their Leaders,* published in 1995 by the Times Mirror Center for the People & the Press.

Statistics on bureaucrats who help the government get out the news come from Stephen Hess, *The Government/Press Connection: Press Officers and Their Offices* (Brookings Institution, 1984). So does the I. F. Stone quotation. The Office of Personnel Management statistic comes from an interview with a staff member, Mike Orenstein. The Jefferson quote is from Leonard W. Levy's classic, now called *Emergence of a Free Press* (Oxford University Press, 1985). For a discussion of pseudo news such as that generated by the government, see Daniel Boorstin, *The Image: A Guide to Pseudo Events in America* (Atheneum, 1961).

A great deal has been written on the shortcomings of U.S. coverage of foreign news. Here are some sources used in this section: Jonathan Power, "Still New Under the Sun: Truth," New York *Times,* November 7, 1975 (which includes the quotes and information on Chile); John Maxwell Hamilton and George Krimsky, "'Juju' News from Abroad," *Gannett Center Journal* (Fall, 1989); Daniel Riffe, "News Items in the 'Shrinking Foreign Newshole': The Case of the New York Times," paper presented at the 1992 meeting of the Association for Education in Journalism and Mass Communications; Sanford Ungar and David Gergen, "Africa and the American Media," Freedom Forum Media Studies Center, Occasional Paper No. 9, November, 1991; John Maxwell Hamilton, "Ho-hum—Latin America," *Columbia Journalism Review* (May/June, 1977).

For background on King George's timely death, see J. H. Rolland Ramsay, "A King, a Doctor, and a Convenient Death," *British Medical*

*Journal,* May 28, 1994. The media critic on the SLA coverage was Desmond Smith, "A New Brand of Terrorism," *Nation,* March 30, 1974. A witty essay about Edward Kennedy breaking the German surrender story ahead of time was written by A. J. Liebling, "The A.P. Surrender," *New Yorker,* May 19, 1945.

Calvin Trillin's article on people-oriented news bias appeared in "U.S. Journal: Houston," *New Yorker,* January 6, 1975. The Helmore letter was written September 8, 1994, to George Krimsky.

The quote from Joseph Mitchell can be found in his delightful volume *My Ears Are Bent* (Sheridan House, 1938). The Harrison Salisbury story is in Gay Talese, *The Kingdom and the Power* (Dell, 1986).

Regarding coverage of the Zoe Baird episode, the Washington *Post's* attitude was explained in an article in that paper by media critic Howard Kurtz, January 23, 1993.

Background on the shooting of one Treasury Department agent by another can be found in Paul M. Hogan, "Ohio: Printing the Obscenity," *Columbia Journalism Review* (July/August, 1975). For the Neuharth "above the fold" quote, see Peter Andrews, "The Press," *American Heritage* (October, 1994). The Detroit *News's* gay column is discussed in its own article, June 2, 1995, by Deb Price and Joyce Murdoch. The Woodstock photo is discussed in "No Nudes Is Good Nudes," *Editor & Publisher,* February 11, 1995. For a funny column on the Los Angeles *Times* guide, read John Leo, "Falling for Sensitivity," *U.S. News & World Report,* December 13, 1993.

# V

Joann Byrd's article is in the Washington *Post,* November 29, 1992.

Much anxiety is expended over the use of anonymous sources. The sources in this book include William B. Blankenburg, "The Utility of Anonymous Attribution," *Newspaper Research Journal* (Winter/Spring, 1992), which describes the frequency with which such sources are used. For differing interpretations of "off the record," see Bruce Porter and Timothy Ferris, *The Practice of Journalism: A Guide to Reporting and Writing the News* (Prentice Hall, 1988); and Daniel R. Williamson, *Newsgathering* (Hastings House, 1979). The Deep Throat story is from Carl Bernstein and Bob Woodward, *All the President's Men* (Simon and Schuster, 1974). Maureen Dowd's quote is from the New York *Times,* May 8, 1994. For the comment on the Cincinnati *Enquirer* story, see George Blake, "Rebuilding Credibility,"

*Quill* (April, 1988). Bradlee is quoted in John Hohenberg, *The Professional Journalist: A Guide to the Practices and Principles of the News Media* (Holt, Rinehart and Winston, 1960). The Bush quote on anonymous sources is in John E. Yang, Washington *Post,* March 13, 1992.

The New York *Times* comment on the Farber case is found in "Forced Disclosure of Confidential Notes," in the *Columbia Journalism Review* (November/December, 1978).

The Newt Gingrich quote is from *Vanity Fair* (July, 1989) and found in *Quotations from Speaker Newt,* ed. Amy D. Bernstein and Peter W. Bernstein (Workman Press, 1995). Nixon's quote on getting the press is in Stephen E. Ambrose, *Nixon: The Triumph of a Politician, 1962-1972* (Simon and Schuster, 1989). Sidey's article appeared as "How I Made the Enemies List," *Time,* June 8, 1987; this article is useful on the enemies list as well as on Kennedy. The McGrory story comes from *New York Times Magazine,* January 1, 1995. Martin Mayer's *Making News* has worthwhile observations on official sources; the 1973 study showing widespread reliance on officials for news was by Leon Sigal and is cited in Mayer's book. The veteran Washington journalist quoted as saying journalists like to be greeted pleasantly is James McCartney; this is found in *Reading the News.* The observation on cops and police reporters getting along is from Robert Darnton, *The Kiss of Lamourette* (Norton, 1990). On the revolving door between politics and journalism, see Jules Witcover, "Revolving-Door Journalists," *Washington Journalism Review* (April, 1990). The story about keeping the atomic bomb secret is from Robert Jay Lifton and Greg Mitchell, *Hiroshima in America: Fifty Years of Denial* (Putnam, 1995).

On use of quotations, see Philip Weiss, "Who Gets Quote Approval?" *Columbia Journalism Review* (May/June, 1991).

The Supreme Court citation on clearing quotes is from *Nebraska Press Association* v. *Stuart,* 1976. See also Steve Weinberg, "So What's Wrong with Pre-Publication Review?" *Quill* (May, 1990).

Ken Mutzler's article "Shooting It Out with the News Media" appeared in the United Airlines magazine *Hemispheres* (March, 1994).

The New York *Daily News*'s purchase of the photo is from Tom Goldstein, *The News at Any Cost: How Journalists Compromise Their Ethics to Shape the News* (Simon and Schuster, 1985). This book provides useful discussion on ethical issues facing journalists.

For examples of financing news stories, see Silas Bent, *Ballyhoo: The Voice of the Press* (Horace Liveright, 1927). On the *National Enquirer,* see Pat Jordan, "Hello. This is Alan Smith of the *National Enquirer,*" *New York Times Magazine,* June 25, 1995.

For a general discussion on purchasing news, see Bruce Selcraig, "Buying News," *Columbia Journalism Review* (July/August, 1994). Also see the *Freedom Forum Weekly* newsletter, July 25, 1994; Lyle Denniston, "Making Checkbook Journalism a Crime," *American Journalism Review* (April, 1995); and "Federal Judge Kills 'Checkbook Journalism' Law in California," *Editor & Publisher,* August 26, 1995. The statistic on televisions in homes in 1952 is from Emery and Emery, *The Press and America.* Bennett's blackmailing is noted in Tucher's *Froth and Scum.*

## VI

Details on newsroom demographics and education levels are found in *The Changing Face of the Newsroom* (American Society of Newspaper Editors, 1989); Weaver and Wilhoit, *The American Journalist in the 1990s;* Lee B. Becker, "Finding Work Was More Difficult for Graduates in 1990," *Journalism Educator* (Summer, 1992); Lee Becker and Joseph Graf, *Myths and Trends: What the Numbers Say About Journalism Education* (Freedom Forum, 1995); and a study commissioned by the Associated Press Managing Editors Association, "Journalist Satisfaction Study" (MORI Research, Minneapolis, 1983). The Bureau of Labor Statistics report on median wages was published in the New York *Times,* May 14, 1995. Breslin's quote appeared in the Washington *Post,* April 4, 1992.

The survey in which media leaders noted a liberal bias among journalists was done by Judith Sylvester, Charles Mayo, and Billy I. Ross in March, 1995, as part of their Media Leaders' Forum studies at Louisiana State University. The other survey on the media's liberal attitudes is *The People, the Press, and Their Leaders,* which was cited earlier and done by Times Mirror. Scripps's quote on wealth is from the Emery history *The Press and America.* For an example of a socialist in the establishment press, see A. Kent Macdougall, "Memoirs of a Radical in the Mainstream Press," *Columbia Journalism Review* (March/April, 1989). Macdougall notes that, despite his views, "I remained a journalist first and a radical second throughout my career."

The McLellan quote is found in an interesting op-ed article on journalists being suckered into stories that are literally too good to be true: Walter Olson, *Wall Street Journal,* March 27, 1995.

For background on increased cynicism about and aggression toward national leaders, see Broder's *Behind the Front Page;* Larry J. Sabato, *Feeding Frenzy: How Attack Journalism Has Transformed American Politics* (Free Press, 1991); Adam Gopnik, "Read All About It," *New Yorker,* December 12, 1994; and Michael Schudson, *Watergate in American Memory* (Basic Books, 1992). The Wilde quote is found in Mitchell Stephens' *History of News.*

Donald E. Skinner's farewell letter to the staff of the Orange County *Register* is cited in the *Columbia Journalism Review* (May/June, 1992); Sesno's quote is from the Sabato book. Harrison Salisbury's description of Roberts came in the *American Journalism Review* (December, 1993).

A good article on prize giving is Eliot Frankel and Mitchell Stephens, "Prize and Prejudice: The Journalism Awards Racket," *Washington Journalism Review* (September, 1991). Also see Bruce Porter, "So What?" *Columbia Journalism Review* (March/April, 1995), which shows how winning prizes does not necessarily further a journalist's career.

The weekly newspaper editor quoted at the end of the section on bylines is Tom Grubisich, editor of *The Connection* newspapers, based in Reston, Virginia.

# VII

Requiring congressional correspondents to disclose outside income is discussed in Debra Gersh Hernandez, *Editor & Publisher,* August 12, 1995. Background on press councils can be found in William L. Rivers, William B. Blankenburg, Kenneth Starck, and Earl Reeves, *Back-Talk: Press Councils in America* (Canfield Press, 1972); Louise Williams Hermanson, "News Council Complainants: Who Are They and What Do They Want?" *Journalism Quarterly* (Winter, 1993); *Editor & Publisher,* April 9, 1994. Examples of National Press Council decisions are from *Columbia Journalism Review* (November/December, 1979).

Background on ombudsmen can be found in John Maxwell Hamilton, *Nation,* March 16, 1974; Richard Harwood, "Media's Liberal Tilt,"

*Nieman Reports* (Winter, 1992); Bill Kirtz, "The Ombudsman: Cost or Benefit?" *Presstime* (June, 1995). Background on various media-watching organizations is provided in "Watchdog Watch," *American Journalism Review* (April, 1993).

Shirley Biagi, *Media Impact: An Introduction to Mass Media* (Wadsworth, 1992), has details on libel judgments as well as the Abrams quote. Also see Barbara Dill, "Libel Law Doesn't Work, But Can It Be Fixed?" in *At What Price? Libel Law and Freedom of the Press* (Twentieth-Century Fund Press, 1993).

Anna Quindlen's column appeared in the New York *Times,* April 12, 1992. Brisbane's quotation is from Chris Spolar, "Privacy for Public Figures," *Washington Journalism Review* (June, 1992), and the Times Mirror Center poll on public perception of privacy is in *The People and the Press* (Times Mirror, 1989). Shepard's article, "Identifying Juvenile Suspects," is in *American Journalism Review* (June, 1994). Overholser is quoted in a Washington *Post* ombudsman column April 23, 1992. For a discussion of Overholser's controversial resignation from the Des Moines *Register,* see the *Wall Street Journal,* September 29, 1995, Howard Kurtz's Washington *Post* column for September 30, 1995, and the article "Editor's Private Life Made Public," *Editor & Publisher,* October 14, 1995.

For background on letters to the editor, both usage and history, see Ernest C. Hynds, "Editorial Page Editors Discuss Use of Letters," *Newspaper Research Journal* (Winter/Spring, 1992); Hynds, "Editors at Most U.S. Dailies See Vital Roles for Editorial Page," *Journalism Quarterly* (Autumn, 1994); and Stephens' *History of News.* The Nevada judge's run-in with the *Daily Sparks Tribune* is described in the New York *Times* February 20, 1995. Readers complaining over the Internet is discussed by Howard Kurtz in the *Washington Post's National Weekly Edition,* July 24–30, 1995.

## VIII

With regard to influence of television, see Tinker and Rukeyser, *Tinker in Television: From General Sarnoff to General Electric* (Simon and Schuster, 1994); *Communique,* May 9, 1995, published by Freedom Forum Media Studies Center; *TV Dimensions '95,* a report by Media Dynamics, Inc.; *Facts About Newspapers, 1995,* published by the Newspaper Association of America; Edwin Diamond, Gregg

Geller, and John Simerman, *National Journal* (December 11, 1993); Thomas Hargrove and Guido H. Stempel, "Where Americans Really Get Their News," a paper read at the Association of Journalism and Mass Communication convention, August, 1995; Larry McGill and Andras Szanto, *Headlines and Sound Bites: Is That the Way It Is?*, published by the Freedom Forum Media Studies Center in 1995. This last study makes an important contribution to the debate over the merits of newspaper versus television news, demonstrating among other things that newspapers are superior when they concentrate on what they do best, not when they ape their electronic competitor. The *Rolling Stone* article appeared on March 5, 1992. The Swope quote is from E. J. Kahn, Jr., *The World of Swope* (Simon and Schuster, 1965).

Neil Postman is worth reading, especially *Technopoly: The Surrender of Culture to Technology* (Vintage, 1993) and *Amusing Ourselves to Death* (Viking, 1985). With regard to literacy, see the National Newspaper Association press release for January 10, 1995; "Newspapers and Illiteracy," *Editor & Publisher,* June 25, 1988; and National Center for Education Statistics published by the U.S. Department of Education (1994). The changing definitions of literacy are described in Shirley Foutz's "Adult Illiteracy: Will Newspapers Take the Lead?" *Ideas* (September, 1992). For stories on newspaper readership, see William Glaberson's article in the New York *Times* January 17, 1994; and Joseph Ungaro, "First the Bad News," *Media Studies Journal* (Fall, 1991).

For history on Pulitzer, see Frank Luther Mott, *American Journalism,* Chap. 26; for a discussion of new features at the turn of the century, see Mott, Chap. 34. The report of the commission headed by Hutchins was cited in the Introduction as *A Free and Responsible Press.* See also Oswald Garrison Villard, *The Disappearing Daily: Chapters in American Newspaper Evolution* (Knopf, 1944).

The two articles in *Editor & Publisher* were published in the "Shop Talk at Thirty" column: Allen Neuharth, February 26, 1994, and James P. Gannon, August 27, 1994.

The quotation on Boca Raton *News* is from an article by Howard Kurtz, Washington *Post,* January 6, 1991.

Many books provide background on the information economy; the Drucker volume is called *Post-Capitalist Society* (HarperBusiness, 1993).

On newspapers and the environment, see Ralph L. Lowenstein's August 12, 1994, speech, published by the Freedom Forum as "The Electronic Newspaper and Journalism Education."

For background on changes in the newspaper industry, see John Maxwell Hamilton, "Areopagitica Redux: In Defense of Electronic Liberties," *Media Studies Journal* (Fall, 1991).

# Index